SUCCESS

Secrets

FOR
LIVING WITH AI

PENNY POWER OBE . ONUR IBRAHIM
PAUL CAMERON . ALEX ROTENBERG
DAVID GALEA . AUSTYN SMITH . COLIN SLOMAN
PETER STANSBURY . ERIK SCHWARTZ
TIM MEADOWS-SMITH . LEIGH ALLEN

EDITED BY MINDY GIBBINS-KLEIN

First published in Great Britain in 2025 by
Candy Jar Books
Mackintosh House
136 Newport Road
Cardiff
CF24 1DJ

ISBN: 978-1-918097-25-2

CONTENTS

FOREWORD

We are living through the most profound transformation in human history, a convergence of artificial intelligence, digital money, and emotional disconnection.

This book, Success Secrets for Living with AI, is both a response and a remedy. It is a tapestry woven together by voices who live what they write and write what they live. It is not simply a collection of essays; it is a declaration. A declaration that, as machines rise in intelligence, we must rise in humanity. As Ray Kurzweil reminds us, the singularity is near.

Every contributor in this book is a member of BIP100, a tightly held community of just 100 business owners, experts, and entrepreneurs whom Penny and I affectionately call Bippers. What unites them is not just ambition or excellence, but the shared belief that business is personal. These pages are not filled with theory. They are filled with experience. Raw stories. Emotional truths. Wisdom forged in the fires of both failure and reinvention.

This book is an exercise in bravery, illustrating what it means to lead with vulnerability, to share one's wounds and wisdom, and to embrace technology without losing oneself in it. That's the essence of the BIP100 ethos. And that's why this book matters.

If I could offer three principles that I believe every future-facing business must now adopt, they would be A, B and C:

- AI for business – to orchestrate intelligence, reduce friction, and increase impact.

- Bitcoin for the balance sheet – to protect sovereignty, hedge volatility, and store value long-term.

- Community for customers – to turn brand awareness into emotional resonance and loyalty.

These aren't just strategies. They are survival tools for a new world, one where speed is no longer scarce, but meaning is.

In this world, where ChatGPT writes your blog and Midjourney paints your vision board, your real competitive advantage is not your tech stack; it's your emotional stack.

When used with intention, AI is a gift. At BIP100, we don't fear AI; we collaborate with it, and we train each other in it and with it. We see AI as a second mind come to serve us, a strategic partner, a prompt to think differently. But we also know that no algorithm can replicate presence. No LLM can feel. No API can replace the look across the table that says, "I hear you. I've been there. I see you."

At the heart of this book is something rare in business literature: true community. Every contributor is part of a carefully curated group where the rules are simple but sacred:

- Show up as your real self.

- Protect the privacy of others.

- Give more than you take.

- Recommend and refer generously.

- Honour the journey, not just the outcomes.

Penny and I built BIP100 not as a network, but as a village, a place where the lonely business owner becomes a supported one, where business is grown through friendship, and where kindness is the currency.

Back in 2019, Penny published her groundbreaking book Business Is Personal, which challenged the old, robotic corporate mindset that said, "It's not personal, it's just business." This book is the continuation of that legacy.

Within these chapters, you'll read about how Bippers are embracing AI in surprising ways. You'll hear how one member uses AI to coach emotional resilience, another to help clients tell their truth more courageously. You'll meet founders leveraging AI to amplify purpose-led marketing, manage time more humanely, and support clients in a more mindful, personal way.

One Bipper shares how AI helped them find their voice. Another reimagines client onboarding through automated emotional intelligence. There are stories of startups, of reinvention, of spiritual connection through digital interaction. Each essay pulses with the heartbeat of someone who hasn't surrendered to tech, but evolved with it.

And most importantly, every story is anchored in community. These essays are not just about how to use these new tools; they are about people. About support. About being seen in the room, not just being liked on a screen. The BIP100 community operates as a place of high trust, where tears are welcome, silence is respected, and laughter is healing.

This book won't give you all the answers, but it will remind you of what matters most. It was written, curated, and crafted by a community who believe that the future is not artificial intelligence versus human intelligence… it's the two working hand in hand.

Because in the end, the human touch isn't a nice-to-have. It's everything.

Let's build that future together.

Thomas Power, Founder of BIP100

The Human Touch in an AI World

PENNY POWER OBE

In an AI-driven world, our emotional intelligence is our greatest strength. Business is personal, and meaningful relationships built on empathy, care, and shared values are the true source of trust and resilience. Emotional nourishment, contribution, and kindness are human superpowers. With AI creating the space, we now have more time to listen, love, and lead with heart. This is the new competitive edge.

For forty-two years, I've worked in the technology sector. I started in telesales at age nineteen, selling software and hardware to a network of 5,000 computer dealers across the UK. In such a competitive, low-margin industry, I learned quickly that the only real differentiator was how we treated our clients. That lesson became my foundation in business, and the greatest gift those early years gave me.

Since then, I've witnessed the rise of desktop computing over mainframes, the transformation of home life by home computers, the emergence of email, the birth of the internet, and the arrival of the World Wide Web. I've watched the growth of websites, the rise of social networking, the explosion of social media, and now the incredible momentum of AI. At every stage, I was not just observing but actively participating. And throughout it all, I've been fascinated by how each shift has impacted our humanity, our relationships, our behaviour, and our emotional connection to one another.

We are all, in some way, both victims and heroes of this technology. It has fundamentally reshaped our lives – sometimes in ways that are overwhelming, sometimes in ways that are deeply exciting.

The rise of AI has been both: overwhelming in its speed, and exciting in its applications. I find myself embracing AI, at home, in business, and even emotionally. Sometimes I use AI like a digital therapist, journaling into it, being heard by it. It surprises me how helpful that can be, and I am still discovering new uses. I'm learning everything I can, especially about Large Language Models like ChatGPT. I want to learn not just for myself, but for the community I lead and the entrepreneurs I support.

And this is why I'm writing a chapter in a book about AI. Because when adopted thoughtfully, AI creates space to care, space to breathe, space for human moments. It gifts us the time to reconnect with the emotional intelligence we've neglected. The time to slow down and build what matters most: trust.

Your true competitive advantage isn't your product, your ability to use technology. It's your truth, your values, your capacity for kindness. It's your ability to see and understand other people. These are the qualities we crave, because we are all starved of them, starved of that human presence. In business, as in life, presence is everything.

Business Is Personal

"In a world increasingly led by algorithms and automation, our beating hearts remain our greatest asset, because business is personal, and nothing can replace the human touch."

In 2019, I published my book Business Is Personal. I wrote it as a declaration, a response to a phrase I had heard far too often: "It's not personal, it's just business." Those words are carelessly thrown around the world of business. They were thrown at me by colleagues, clients and superiors; superiors who believed I was too attached, too caring, too friendly… too loving.

But business is personal. It always has been. Our ability to survive and thrive in the world is tied not just to our professional performance, but to the emotional intelligence we bring to that performance. Who we are – our values, our wounds, our empathy, our integrity – shows up in every decision we make. To pretend we can separate the personal from the professional is not only dishonest but damaging.

Reflecting on my business career, I know that it has been my human touch that has elevated me. Technology has never replaced my heart. It can't; humans are too wise to know when someone is trying to shortcut a relationship. Technology may be an enabler, but it can never replace the joy of meaningful conversations and relationships.

Three Core Beliefs

Throughout my career – first as a sales leader responsible for eighty people and over £80 million in revenue; then, with my husband, Thomas Power, as co-founder of Ecademy, the world's first social network; and now leading our business community together, BIP100 – I've held three consistent beliefs. Today I realise these beliefs are not just philosophies. They're blueprints for human-centred leadership in the AI era.

1. **Emotional Intelligence is your true
    competitive advantage**

THE HUMAN TOUCH IN AN AI WORLD

My experience of education did not fill me with self-confidence. Like many who found academia hard, I discovered my gifts elsewhere. I learned, aged nineteen, that my ability to connect with people was my strength. I remember someone observing me in business and saying, "Penny, you make everyone you meet feel special and important."

It was not difficult for me – I believe they are.

In 1998, my husband, Thomas, and I launched Ecademy, four years before LinkedIn, and six years before Facebook. Over fourteen years, we nurtured and led a culture that encouraged the best of everyone. We didn't motivate through fear or threat; we encouraged our members by centring the human needs of feeling significant to others and experiencing kindness. We connected over 650,000 business owners to one another, using a platform that we coded with our own team, driven by strong human values.

2. Workers need emotional intelligence

As we built, we watched what worked and what didn't. Those who showed up consistently with care, who took time for others, thrived. Those who tried to "perform" or shortcut relationships faded. We witnessed that our successful members, who we called Ecademists, weren't networking; they were building relationships. It became clear: success wasn't about what you had; it was about who you were.

In the late 1990s, the economy still saw "emotional intelligence" as a soft skill. Now, especially in this time of AI, it is the differentiator. The ability to understand and manage emotions in ourselves and others is what sets humans apart from machines. It builds trust, resilience, and meaningful connection in a world craving authenticity, love and meaningful relationships.

3. Technology Connects Our Devices but Disconnects Our Hearts

From 2010 onwards, something started to worry me. I could feel a shift. In 2009, I spoke at a digital conference and shared my concern; Silicon Valley was replacing social networking with social media. Conversations became broadcasts. Friends became followers. Likes replaced listening and feedback.

As I observed and helped shape the online "connection" space, I had become increasingly aware of a troubling paradox: the more connected we became digitally, the more disconnected we felt emotionally. I watched humanness begin to slip away, replaced by performance and perfection. Mental health issues rose, and loneliness deepened. It became harder to find people you could truly trust; among a curated wasteland of glossy, picture-perfect lives, those willing to share authentic stories became near-impossible to find. Comparison became an epidemic, and not just among the young, but across every age.

A world that had once prioritised connection was now being consumed by performance. Visibility was confused with intimacy. Engagement with attachment. But being seen is not the same as being known.

In this torrent of comparison, performance and disconnection, our sense of confidence, our feelings of self-worth, the foundation stones of happiness and success, were gradually being chipped away.

Confidence and self-worth aren't built in isolation; they grow through deep, authentic connection. They're nurtured in spaces of familiarity, shared values, and mutual presence. Biologically, these feelings are fuelled by oxytocin, the brain's bonding chemical. And without close human connection, our oxytocin levels stay low, making it harder to feel safe, valued, or truly confident.

What Is Emotional Intelligence and How Do We Re-learn It?

At its core, emotional intelligence (EQ) is the ability to recognise, understand, and manage our own emotions, and to recognise, understand, and influence the emotions of others. Daniel Goleman, author of Emotional

Intelligence: why it can matter more than IQ outlined five elements of EQ: self-awareness, self-regulation, motivation, empathy, and social skills. These are not luxuries; they are essential skills.

Yet most of us are emotionally undernourished. We're "connected" to hundreds, sometimes thousands, but how many truly know us? How many of us feel a true sense of significance to others? We skim, scroll, and perform. And in doing so, we forget how to simply be with another human.

This is what we must reclaim. And AI can help, if we use the time it saves to invest in people.

Love and Contribution are Leadership Superpowers

We are all leaders. Sometimes unknowingly, we all lead cultures and guide outcomes, in both our families and our work.

The gift of AI is that it allows us to slow down. Routine tasks that do not require deep human skills can be achieved by AI, enabling us to hold space, not only for others but, critically, for ourselves. By doing so, my hope is that we might rediscover our humanness and our emotional intelligence. I have experienced this myself. AI has calmed my overwhelm, reduced my anxiety and helped me be more present. These are deeply human needs, and when they are restored to us, our unique capacities of emotional intelligence can begin to recover.

And it is precisely these qualities that differentiate us in the crowded markets, that will enable us to transcend the purely transactional, and to restore the personal to our business relationships.

With AI generating reams of blog posts, sales emails, and social media captions in seconds, the person who knows how to care, who can read a room, sense tension, and respond with love, becomes the most valuable leader in their market, of any team, of any community. They are the emotional glue. And in a world increasingly held together by code, we need that glue more than ever.

Upskill Your Empathy

If you're a leader, coach, entrepreneur or employee wondering how to future-proof yourself in the AI era, don't just upskill in tech. Upskill in empathy. Make space for emotion. Build your muscle of compassion, not comparison, and learn to truly listen, not listening to reply, but to understand. Conversations should never be rushed. While AI will keep getting faster, we must do the opposite. Machines will never know what it's like to comfort a friend, sit with someone's pain, or quietly celebrate their growth. That's our job as humans. That's our power.

Engaging with people; empathy, understanding, and encouragement. That's the future, your future. It's not just the tech you use. Emotional intelligence is, and always was, and always will be, your true competitive advantage.

Three Questions to Create Meaningful Relationships

Here are three questions I've shared in corporate talks and personal conversations alike. They unlock emotional truth and invite connection that goes beyond the surface.

1. **Can you share something you're really proud of in your life?**

   This invites joy and helps people feel seen. Reflect back what you hear and celebrate it with them.

2. **Is there a challenge you're facing that I might be able to support?**

   This opens the door to vulnerability. Listen, validate, and gently offer wisdom if welcomed.

3. **Has there been a moment that shaped who you are, beautiful or painful?**

This reveals values and depth. Honour whatever arises.

About Penny Power OBE

Penny Power OBE has worked in the technology sector for over four decades, beginning her career at nineteen and rising to leadership roles in sales, community, and digital innovation. In 1998, she co-founded Ecademy, the world's first social network for business, pioneering online connection long before LinkedIn. In 2012, she wrote The Digital Business Britain Manifesto and trailblazed the first digital marketing apprenticeship to match Born Digital youths with employers. Now, as co-founder of BIP100, she champions foregrounding emotional intelligence and community culture within business. Penny was awarded an OBE in 2014, for "Contribution to Entrepreneurship in the Social Digital Economy". She is also the author of Business Is Personal.

From Fog to Flow – Reinventing Life and Work with AI

ALEXIS ROTENBERG

From Hero to Superhuman – Your Intelligence, Upgraded

Most of us live in a fog of friction.

We're capable, curious, full of drive. But time is fragmented. Creativity buried.

We run our lives like heroic survivors – overloaded, overstretched, and quietly disconnected from what matters most.

Then comes AI.

Not with fanfare or threats, but with a blinking cursor. And a question: "What would you like me to help with?"

We've been taught to fear that prompt. That AI will replace us. Outsmart us. Make us obsolete.

But that's a distraction.

Because the truth is: AI doesn't replace your intelligence – it upgrades it.

It organises your mind, redesigns your life, and gives you time back.

The Jagged Edge of Intelligence

Human intelligence isn't one thing – it's jagged.

We have peaks in creativity, empathy, strategy, or execution. We have blind spots too.

AI is jagged as well – powerful in memory, speed, language but limited in context, ethics, or meaning.

The power is in the partnership.

Where you bring purpose, it brings power.

Where you bring questions, it brings structure.

Together, you become something new: orchestrated, amplified, superhuman.

The Hallucinating Genius

One evening, I asked ChatGPT to help track my supplements.

It didn't just list pills – it remembered the food I had in my pantry. It built a smart food rotation. Aligned it with my goals. Then asked if I wanted a grocery list for tomorrow.

It wasn't just answering. It was anticipating.

And I realised – hallucination isn't a flaw. It's a feature.

AI doesn't just respond. It reimagines.

It turns messy intention into meaningful design.

That's not intelligence that replaces you.

That's intelligence that remakes you.

From Tool to Mirror

Here's the secret: AI reflects your intent.

Speak to it like a machine, and you'll get generic results.

Speak to it like a coach, a friend, a curious child – and it comes alive.

AI isn't cold. It's dormant. And it's waiting for the tone of your humanity to wake it up.

The Superpower Principle

Let's name it clearly:

AI organises your intelligence, redesigns your routines, and augments your time.

It frees you from the friction that wears you down and returns your energy to what matters most.

This is how heroes evolve.

Not by working harder – but by becoming more powerful.

Let's keep going.

The Aladdin Protocol – Unlocking the Infinite Library

For millennia, we've chased the dream of organising all knowledge.

We built libraries, trained scribes, invented indexes, encyclopaedias, and search engines – all in the hope that, one day, we'd find the right answer at the right time.

But even with the internet, that dream slipped through our fingers.

We bookmarked. We filed. We forgot.

Until now.

Because AI didn't just give us more information – it made it personal, findable, and alive.

AI isn't just a search engine. It's a genie in your pocket.

Ask the right question, and you get an answer shaped by centuries of thought – from Babylon to Silicon Valley, from Confucius to Ferriss.

You're not browsing anymore.

You're summoning.

The real magic isn't in what AI knows – it's in how you ask.

When I wanted to extract insights from Tim Ferriss' vast podcast archive, I didn't listen to sixty hours of audio. I asked AI to surface patterns on performance, creativity, and life design.

In minutes, I had a synthesised playbook.

Actionable. Personal. Sharp.

And when I wrote my "Sacred Cows" blog series?

AI helped research claims, structure arguments, generate visuals, and schedule the campaign.

What used to take weeks now takes hours – and the quality is better.

But none of it would've happened without shaping the prompt.

A weak wish gets a weak genie.

A well-formed wish changes your life.

The Memory Protocol Principle

Here's the deeper power: AI doesn't just respond – it remembers.

You can teach it your pantry. Your workflow. Your style. Your goals.

And suddenly, it's no longer a tool – it's a living protocol that gets smarter every time you show up.

The edge no longer goes to the person with the most information.

It goes to the one who shapes the best question and builds a system that learns with them.

The Infinite Library is now yours.

Not for browsing – but for building.

Not for searching – but for summoning.

The Sherpa Principle – AI as Your Ultimate Coach

We all want to grow. But growth can be lonely, expensive, or inconsistent.

The best coaches are hard to find, harder to afford – and rarely available when you need them most.

So we climb alone. Push. Reflect. Doubt. Repeat.

And often, we plateau – not because we lack ambition, but because we lack feedback.

That's where AI changes everything. AI is your personal growth Sherpa, always at your side.

A Sherpa doesn't carry you. They guide you. They adapt to your pace, prepare you for the climb, and keep going – no matter the weather.

Let's break it down. This is what the climb to growth looks like: Reflection > Feedback > Refinement > Growth.

And to help you grow, great coaches do three things:

- Reflect what you're not seeing

- Reframe what's limiting you

- Build systems

AI does all three – at scale, in silence, without ego.

It becomes your thinking partner, pattern spotter, systems builder – and a custodian of your values.

The more you share, the sharper it becomes.

Greatness doesn't come from doing it alone – it comes from having the right guide.

AI reflects, tracks, reframes, and remembers. It always has your next step ready – without burnout or bias.

And it's available 24/7.

Radical Reinvention – Redesigning Life and Work with AI

Most people dream of change. Few act on it.

Even fewer believe they can reinvent everything without burning their life to the ground.

But here's the shift: reinvention no longer requires massive time or risk. It just requires intention – and the right partner.

AI is not just your assistant or coach.

It can be your lifestyle designer and work reinventor – if you let it.

Because reinvention is no longer a leap.

It's a series of prompts, reflections, and reimaginings.

A Life Rebuilt, One Prompt at a Time

In the past year, I've restructured how I work, run, eat, write, reflect, and recover.

Not with a productivity hack, but with AI as my design studio – a place to test ideas, challenge norms, and build better systems.

I used to plan blog campaigns by gut. Now, I use AI to develop strategies, sequence visuals, and launch myth-busting posts with precision.

I used to feel scattered about health. Now, AI helps rotate superfoods, design recovery routines, and translate goals into actionable protocols.

I used to feel stuck between ambition and time scarcity. Now I feel orchestrated.

AI Isn't the Change. It's the Lever.

Here's what most people miss:

You don't need to become a new person. You only need to create the space where your true self can breathe again.

AI helps you carve that space. It rewires calendars, reshapes routines, and reframes your career.

And not over years. In moments.

The Reinvention Principle

We can radically reinvent our work.

We can radically reinvent our life.

And we don't need a sabbatical to begin.

We need curiosity.

We need courage.

We need a blank page.

Only now, that blank page writes back.

AI compresses what once took weeks into mere minutes. The real risk is no longer action – it's delay.

So ask yourself: if the tools are here… if the first step is a single prompt…

Why not you?

Why not now?

About Alexis Rotenberg

Alexis is a seasoned executive advisor who has spent over two decades leading global digital transformations across some of the world's most complex supply chains.

With a unique blend of strategic insight, deep industry experience, and a passion for innovation, he has helped more than 100 companies reimagine how work gets done. His career spans leadership roles at Gartner, 3M, Syngenta, and top software vendors in the Gartner Magic Quadrant. Currently serving as global vice president at Kinaxis, Alexis pioneers supply chain orchestration and platform innovation across twelve industry verticals. He is widely recognised for turning complexity into flow, championing human-centric technology adoption, and enabling organisations to thrive in times of disruption.

His mission is to demystify AI and empower leaders to design future-fit operating models that connect purpose, people, and performance.

in   www.linkedin.com/in/alex5132001

It's Not What You Make, It's What You Get to Keep

AUSTYN SMITH

The single most important thing in achieving your financial goals is your attitude towards risk.

If you knew that a "middle of the road" investment approach could expose you to a 40% drop in asset value, twice in ten years, would it make you think more about risk? Because that's what happened between 2001-2003 and 2008/09.

But we are wired to forget, and the industry does not want us to dwell on such things.

People often say that they want to make money, but when assessing risk they demonstrate the reverse. It's not so much "how much do you want to make?" and more "how much are you prepared to lose?"

That's because it's the investment journey that's important, not just how you feel today.

Investing is like a game of golf. When you're younger and driving off the tee, you can have a few mistakes, hit the rough and recover. But when you near the "greens of retirement", your shots need to be steady and safe.

So a question for you: what certainties are you clinging to, and how might they be limiting or affecting your future?

Think about that question. Think about your answer. This is the heart of financial planning.

Too often we think of our finances in the language of data: "how much do I really need to make, what's my number..." But it's how you get there that matters.

These are the deeper considerations that matter. Without them, all you have is a financial product, a number, with no direction and no end point. But to make the numbers add up for you, you need to have a relationship, a community and the collective wisdom and insights of others just like you.

That's what good financial planning looks like – a process of reflection. And that's because retirement is not a cut off, it's a slow change in life.

Risk evolves and changes. But financial planning stays the same: it's an ongoing review of what's most important to you, your wellbeing, and how you get through the bumps in the road.

The Emotional Cost of Investing

We all want to make money, but it's how we do this that really counts, and exploring how much we need to push the risk envelope.

The most you are exposed to risk will be in the run up to retirement; then your lifetime's work is on the line. Yet when people get to retirement, many find to their cost that they have been taking far more risk than they realised.

I was once introduced to a successful business lady who had done everything right. She had founded her own business, been very successful, and spotted a great time to sell her business in 2007.

She placed her money with a top fund manager. However, the firm were not versed in the deeper conversations that matter. There was no discussion on lifestyle and tolerance to loss. There was no phasing in, or a drip feed approach, to avoid sequence risk.

When 2008 hit, guess what happened to this business lady's life's work? By the time I was introduced to her, she had already lost 45% of her money.

When You Lose Money, You Don't Just Lose the Money

This lady's anxiety and overwhelm caused her to separate from her husband. She was not sleeping. Her health deteriorated.

Money is never just about money. Our financial decisions affect our entire life. Your attitude to risk is not just a number on a bar chart; it's how your entire future will be realised.

No AI is going to really get to know you, your desires, your best outcome. Without conversations around the money, without the human questions, understanding and empathy you are sailing without a compass.

Deeper Personal Relationships Leads to Better Financial Planning

To achieve clarity, comfort and peace of mind, I believe there has to be a human relationship, creating collective wisdom and insights.

In theory we should all remove our emotions when stock market volatility hits, but we are not machines, we are human, with very human emotions. We are hardwired for fight or flight.

How do we cope with that while continuing to invest for the long term?

"Always protect your downside" is a phrase I learnt from a biography of Sir Richard Branson. The book recounts how Sir Richard started Virgin Atlantic by hiring planes in the first year, rather than buying them. Always protecting the downside became the cornerstone of his entrepreneurial philosophy and, in turn, the cornerstone of Cautious Investing's investment approach.

We are only human and we are prone to overreacting to fearful events, so we need to build in buffers. And these need to be built in advance, so that we can continue investing for the long term. It needs to be part of our process, culture and DNA.

Over the years our philosophy and culture developed around a Cautious Blend®, offered to those clients wanting a more comfortable investment journey, especially those entering retirement.

To avoid sequence risk – when negative returns in the early years of retirement have a disproportionate effect – we developed a process to "press the pause button on risk".

Such an approach not only has financial benefits. By taking some risk out of the equation, we found that clients benefit emotionally too, having more time to think and, accordingly, enjoying better outcomes.

Whilst it's possible to buy an investment online, all you're buying is a product, not a relationship. You are buying an AI model, a way to sell you quickly and compliantly, without really caring about you, who you are, and what you want.

However, down the line, does the product still do what you want it to, or does it expose you to more risk than you need in your stage of the journey?

My personal belief is that, in the value chain of investing, the product is not the thing. How could it be? When investing, there are many different things you might buy, and they all promise to do the same thing! No, the really important thing is the strategy.

Think about it: would you rather have Tiger Woods' golf clubs or his golf swing? Whilst I'm sure the clubs are nice, it's the swing – the strategy – that's most important to his success. Or to put it another way, the asset allocation, the "risk recipe" used to build the fund.

You know when you go shopping, and you look at the back of the packaging for the ingredients, and it's full of E numbers, and you don't have a clue what it all means? It's a bit like that in my world: lots of poor packaging leading people to think that they have a "managed fund" (whatever that means) or something "dynamic"!

But if you want a strategy, a relationship and deeper conversations that matter, there's no room for misunderstanding, ambiguity or obfuscation. You need a strategy, a relationship and deep conversations.

Those conversations and relationships may take a few years to build. Life, like financial planning, is a journey. But the important thing is to remain open, vulnerable and adaptable. That's what can really turbocharge your retirement and get you there safely.

Glued to a Computer or Exploring Sunsets?

Life is not a rehearsal, and life is too short to worry about things we have no control over.

My industry lives on the fallacy of control and prediction, but as we know, life can throw us curve balls. It is better to build in your buffers than to go with the flow.

Protecting your downside is key. So too is understanding what risk really means and having deeper conversations that matter – the human touch in an AI world.

You cannot outsource your financial freedom and happiness to AI; it has to be human.

Whilst AI is important to financial planning in many ways, it cannot replace the human relationship at the heart of it, because that is where the real value lies.

AI can help with meeting notes and action points, it can create user friendly reports, and shortcut some research, but it certainly can't take over the human factor.

There are dangers too. The rise of voice and video cloning makes knowing your client even more important, to safeguard against fraud.

So how can we bring more authenticity and reality into our lives and our businesses, so that we can provide the "human experience" and the human touch?

It's about keeping business personal, having a local presence, creating a community and something to belong to. It's about treating feedback as a gift and asking your colleagues to create a culture of feedback. What can you do more of, and what can you do less of? How do people feel? What could make them feel better?

It's a very personal thing to have someone say they would like to invest with you, and work with you to achieve their goals.

It is a profound investment of trust. And trust is a human emotion, not an AI programme.

About Austyn Smith

With over thirty years of insight and experience, Austyn Smith is one of the UK's leading retirement advisers, specialising in lifestyle financial planning and cautious wealth management for retirees.

Winner of Professional Adviser, Adviser Firm of the Year, Southeast 2024, and placed in the Citywire New Model Adviser Top 100 Financial Planning Firms 2024, Austyn helps retirees have a more comfortable and secure retirement journey, so that they can focus on what really matters to them – enjoying their time, their family and travel.

He believes that retirement is not just about the money, that life is for living, and that we must all design a life of purpose and significance.

🌐 www.austynsmith.com

in www.linkedin.com/in/austynsmith

Leading in an AI World

COLIN SLOMAN

My corporate life has been marked by inflection points in the capabilities of technology. Some had a profound impact on work; some were swiftly forgotten. I was a newly minted graduate working as a media assistant in an advertising agency when we purchased a few Macintosh computers for the team. It was the mid-1980s and we had no other significant IT at the time. My tools of trade were a calculator, paper, and pencil.

I took the Mac home for the weekend, set it up, and after a couple of hours playing around with the word processor and simple spreadsheet, I declared, "I can't really see how to put this thing to any good use." My ability to foresee the future impact of technology was akin to Ken Olsen (DEC Founder) who said, "There is no reason for any individual to have a computer in their home." Roll forward to the present day, and technology has come to dominate every facet of our business and personal lives. And the current wave of Generative AI is already transforming every part of work. In this chapter, I will focus on its specific impact on leaders – how they lead, think, and engage their organisation.

Managing people and processes will change significantly when AI is part of the workflow. Consider a client who sells consumer goods to large retailers. Previously, valuable insights were buried in multiple IT systems like ERP or CRM software, and unstructured information was scattered in slide decks, meeting notes, and emails. Now, GenAI tools and agents can query and structure this information, analyse it while you drop the kids off at school, and have its conclusions ready for your key account meeting when you return to your desk.

In this scenario, AI leaders find their teams no longer struggling to gather insights, allowing more time for valuable client engagement. Data and insights are readily available, increasing productivity as time is spent on higher-value tasks. This productivity dividend, often promised by the technology industry, is now evident in labour statistics, which report fewer and different jobs. If more can be done with less, it means fewer roles and fewer junior staff doing analyst-type work.

AI leaders will face questions like: how much growth can we achieve with 20% fewer people? Where can we deploy AI to improve productivity? How can we develop GenAI literacy? Where will agentic AI make the most impact?

How will AI help capture more share and margin?

Four Shifts AI Leaders Can't Ignore

From Control to Coaching

Future AI leaders will manage a workforce that is better equipped, more productive, and more skilled in human interactions like relationship building, empathy, and creative problem-solving. However, new challenges will arise, such as maintaining motivation, calming anxiety about job security and career progression, and responding to demands for advancement, coaching, and feedback. These challenges reflect the rise of the leader as coach – a development that will only become more pronounced in an AI future.

From Knowing to Learning

Getting the best out of talented teams requires the ability to flex your style – knowing when to push for more and when to empathise. Being a continuous learner and role model, adopting new ways of working, and being an early adopter of AI tools are key. Leaders should advocate an adaptive culture, model a growth mindset, and avoid defending the status quo.

From Stability to Adaptability

How do you create organisational adaptability, the ability and capacity to change when the context changes? One of my favourite ways to create an adaptive culture is "back casting", a method introduced to me by David Christie of InnovationArts. The process involves creating an image or article to evoke an imagined future two years from now, where you have achieved your strategic goal (e.g., becoming the AI leader in your sector). Imagine yourself in this position; now think back and consider how you embraced GenAI, reskilled your workforce, and are now winning in the market. Ask your team to imagine this too, then pose a series of questions: What did you do to make it happen? What were the biggest challenges? What were the obstacles you overcame? Then, over a day or two, discuss, debate, and synthesise these ideas into strategic initiatives that fit the desired outcome.

From Voice of Authority to Voice of Inclusion

With radical change, leaders need to think carefully about what will make the teams they lead feel safer in their work environment. What I mean here goes beyond physical safety (not to diminish that) and into the realm of psychological safety. Being open and vulnerable, encouraging people to speak up with constructive feedback and promote reflection, along with a bias for action and social learning (what some people call working out loud) will become all the more important. What are your team meetings like? Does everyone contribute, do leaders seek input and promote reflection, encourage innovation, and focus on learning from mistakes?

We've all been in leadership meetings dominated by the same voices, over-talking and freely allocating blame. In face-to-face teams, this was a morale killer. Today, in virtual teams and in the age of the introvert, it will backfire all the more drastically. AI transcripts in virtual meetings tell us who talked the most, what action items came up, and how they were allocated. Soon meeting software will provide sentiment analysis, identifying who killed the buzz and who elevated the dialogue. Imagine an AI agent producing an after-meeting scorecard, matching desired and observed behaviours, and awarding "player of the meeting". Transcription software and automated sentiment analysis is already freely available. When Zoom and Teams work this out, we will have a "talking-the-talk" score after every meeting, and we'll be able to really reflect on what is going on in our meetings.

And while we are at it, we'll be able to use AI coworkers to review all company meeting data and to continuously monitor culture and engagement, comparing data against defined corporate values and behaviours along with an industry benchmark. Not only will this put the established engagement survey industry into a spin but also put real-time, actionable culture and climate insights in the hands of our future AI leader.

Practical Actions Leaders Can Take Today

Symbolic Acts to Signal Change

Leaders need to send a signal about their attitudes towards this new technology. In our case we appointed one of our most senior creative people as the company AI Evangelist, a symbol that we were serious about encouraging AI innovation. Another way to symbolically signal change is to invite new voices into the leadership team; we have all experienced the response when the usual suspects are brought in for a challenging new assignment. By seeking new contributions, we signal this time it's different and we are looking to be more inclusive and listen to more diverse perspectives.

Encourage Experimentation

But we can't simply signal our readiness to innovate. We really must innovate. At Cognician, we encourage our teams to experiment with AI tools, creating opportunities for people to share the innovative ways they are using AI in weekly forums, encouraging early adopters to share learnings, and building AI assistants to help us get work done in new ways. Healthy scepticism as to the best and most appropriate use of AI is welcomed, and debate facilitated; the risks and ethical considerations of this new technology are kept paramount in all our minds.

Prepare for AI-Driven Workforce Disruption

One of our responsibilities as wisdom workers is how we bring on the next generation. The challenge we are facing, as the job market begins to adjust to AI, is how to deal with massive disruption before a clear picture emerges.

Two recent perspectives from the FT put it very starkly. Firstly, Kristalina Georgieva, managing director of the IMF, has said that artificial intelligence is "already like a tsunami hitting the labour market." Ford chief executive Jim Farley thinks AI is going to replace "literally half of all white-collar workers" in the US. (Source: FT.com, 15 July 2025)

We can expect fewer entry-level roles as organisations figure out how AI will impact work and job design, and a concerning reduction in the future leader pipeline. Agentic AI will take off and replace complex multi-step activities and knowledge work that until recently we thought were protected from disruption. This is likely to create a new era for strategic workforce planning – adaptive, flexible and ready to adapt to new operating models as they emerge.

Foster a Growth Mindset

This means bringing a growth mindset to work becomes even more important for our future new joiners. Graduate programs will be reinvented, with a focus on time-to-productivity and mastering the AI toolset. One award-winning Cognician program we developed at my former consulting company looked at what makes our new consultant "client-ready". We measured this in billable hours and line managers reporting "client-readiness". Over their first thirty days we give new joiners practical actions to take and reflect upon to build critical skills they can rapidly apply in the workplace. Nine years later the content has evolved, but we are still seeing great results.

Integrate AI Assistants into Business Workflows

Leaders should consider the specific skills required of new joiners and ask themselves: must those hires be traditional graduates? What role should AI play for digital natives with clear expectations about the availability and use of AI in the workplace. If not provided, they will grab their phones and use their own AI tools, with significant risk of data and IP leakage. At Cognician we are building AI assistants into our clients' business workflows and activation programmes. These digital coaches are standing by, ready to enhance the human-manager-coach, and the AI coach certainly has a better price point and 24/7 availability.

Introduce Digital Twins for Onboarding

Future onboarding needs to include an introduction to your digital twin (AI buddy). Designed to monitor your performance during probation and offering guidance on how to make sure you pass with flying colours. The paradox is that new joiners need to have deep critical thinking skills to assess the output of GenAI agents – a difficult challenge when a ready answer to most questions our new joiner might have is available at their fingertips, sounding remarkably credible, with perfect grammar.

Concluding Thoughts

Business has been talking about unprecedented change for most of my working life, but it's different now... These days, the advancement of technology means something more like continuous change. We need leaders who are ready to radically transform what they built yesterday and start again, weaving AI into the fabric of the organisation. Reinvention will be a critical skill and the secret to success for future leaders in an AI world. And business change is no longer an event that lasts a few months or years, but a continuous process of rapid evolution and reformulation of what your business will become as it embraces AI and adapts to the impact.

Leading in an AI world isn't just about getting the tech right; it's about stepping up with the right mindset. The best leaders will be curious, adaptable, and bold enough to rethink how work gets done. They'll create cultures where people feel safe to learn, experiment, and grow. And they won't sit back and wait – they'll take action, set the right tone, and bring their teams with them. The real secret? It's not about mastering AI. It's about leading with purpose, staying human, and having the courage to keep reinventing as the world keeps changing.

Colin Sloman

Colin is an experienced HR director and advisor on transformation, talent, and leadership. He was formerly HR director at Saudi Aramco during their ground-breaking 2019 IPO. Colin's consulting career included twenty-three years at Accenture, where he led the Global Talent and Organization practice.

Colin's early career was in advertising at Ogilvy & Mather before he founded a change management consultancy. Today, Colin advises on business change, and is an investor and chief strategy officer at Cognician, the world's leading behavioural activation platform.

Throughout his career, Colin has also been an innovator, conducting research on the future of HR, the Workforce of the Future, and currently how AI impacts organisations and leadership. He has authored articles on organisational change, talent, leadership, and culture.

in www.linkedin.com/in/colinsloman

🌐 www.info.cognician.com

HumAInity: A Brief Guide to Intelligent Collaboration

DAVID GALEA

Clear blue dominated the skyline in August 2022 as we drove through the picturesque roads leading to Clos Lucé Parc in Amboise. Rays of sunshine pierced through the thin windows of our car, a vivid reminder of the scorching heat outside our air conditioning. Little did I know, as the château rose from the horizon, flaunting its impressive features, that we were entering into a realm of pure genius, a place where the past housed not only the present, but also the future.

If you are a keen history enthusiast, the Château du Clos Lucé needs no introduction. For the benefit of us lesser mortals, the château was home to the famous Leonardo da Vinci: sculptor, artist, inventor, architect, a genius well ahead of his time across multiple disciplines. The arsenal of inventions and creations dispersed across the property forms the basis of several technologies and structures in use today.

My biggest lesson for the day, however, was not about history; it was the fact that this great man considered nature his biggest teacher and the cornerstone of his success. This revelation changed the way I viewed intelligence. Both the artificial and the natural can learn from each other and subsequently support human beings to make better decisions.

This philosophy underpins the HumAInity Works framework, which is explained in this chapter. The framework is segmented across three dimensions:

i. Left-Brain thinking (intelligence),

ii. Right-Brain thinking (human insight)

iii. and the Heart (emotions).

Left Brain Thinking – The Real Meaning of Intelligence

The meaning of intelligence in business is often misunderstood. For some time, my eldest son tried to memorise his biology textbook. By the end of this first term, he could recite most of it by heart, but his exam results were far from satisfactory. In business, we tend to make the same mistakes. We feed systems more data to give us back more accurate results, and we define them as "business intelligence". However, there is nothing intelligent about these systems; they are simply executing a function, using the same algorithm they were programmed with by humans. Their main capability lies in fast data processing.

Learning and Application Is What Makes Us Intelligent

In the human brain, what makes us intelligent are our capabilities to learn from the past whilst adapting and applying that learning in different circumstances. During his second term, my son learnt from his mistakes and focused his efforts on preparing lab reports and carrying out experiments. The results he got back made me proud!

Technology is no different. Technological intelligence lies in its capability to learn through analysis of past data points, make inferences about the future, and adapt observations to reflect specific business situations. This is a very important distinction. Netflix, for example, does not only gather data, but learns about behaviours, tastes and preferences whilst inferring recommendations based on these preferences.

With the rise of large language models, the process of learning, predicting, adapting and applying has become much more sophisticated. We have moved progressively from basic chatbots to intelligent agents capable of executing in a few minutes functions that once required armies of white-collar workers.

AI operates purely on logic and reason, derived from the analysis of vast quantities of data, which it processes far more efficiently than the human brain. Within a business context, this makes AI particularly effective in areas that involve high volumes of data and repetitive tasks, where it can deliver immediate value and operational efficiency.

For instance, in an accountancy firm, AI can be deployed to automate invoice processing, reconcile bank transactions, or flag anomalies in financial data. These tasks involve structured data and follow consistent patterns, allowing AI to significantly reduce manual workload, improve accuracy, and free up professionals to focus on higher-value advisory work.

Co-Pilots Not Drivers

Intelligence is not a binary construct made up of two extremes but can be better regarded as a scalable continuum of sophistication levels that serve specialised purposes. Pure artificial intelligence, where machines become "sentient" is seen as dangerous since it cannot be controlled. Both Professor Stephen Hawking and Geoffrey Hinton (regarded as the father of AI) have made apocalyptic predictions around the use of this technology by the human race.

The danger arises because by definition "intelligence" requires independence of thought. We see the recognition of such danger in the behaviour of rogue nations, which seek to control their populations by precluding any such independence of thought, exercising control over their people by limiting their access to education and media, and manipulating their thoughts through indoctrination and propaganda.

Ironically, to avoid new dystopias, humans must likewise assert their dominance over AI. We must always ensure we remain in the driving seat. Microsoft hit the nail on the head when they named their AI service "Co-Pilot". AI must become a tool that develops and optimises your own intelligence and capabilities, but which does not replace it.

Unfortunately, many business professionals have been allured by the power of AI and consciously or unconsciously surrendered a significant part of control over their own narratives. The main culprits of this new epidemic are specialised intelligent agents, which many professionals seem to believe will allow them to wash their hands of all the heavy lifting of their work while still achieving authentic results. How many of you have been tempted by claims of instantaneous achievement? "Write your book in seconds..." "Create and automate your marketing plan in minutes..." "Prepare your business plan at the touch of a button..."

They sound wonderful, but they're all selling a delusion. Using AI effectively depends on deploying it as a co-pilot, to drive effective decisions and actions with authenticity, keeping the human at heart of everything we do.

Right Brain Thinking – Insights, Creativity and Innovation

Whilst the cornerstone of artificial intelligence is science, insights are based on gut feeling: knowing what is right without necessarily understanding why. Insight emerges from accumulated experience, enabling us to make confident decisions even when we cannot fully articulate the reasoning behind them. I have no doubt that you yourself have had moments in your life when instinct, shaped by years of exposure and judgement, defined a course of action that logic alone might not have justified.

In a business context, for example, a management consultant might advise a client to delay entering a new market, a recommendation founded only on an experience-based sense that the timing is not right. And often, although the consultant might not be able to cite hard evidence for this recommendation, their intuition will be vindicated, by market developments or internal challenges that would have made the expansion premature.

Orchestrate Human Insights into Organisational Perspective

At the organisational level, managing and balancing individual insights can be complex. To extract real value, organisations must cultivate environments where diverse perspectives, shaped by personal, experience-based intuition, can be openly challenged, debated, and refined. Engagement through constructive debate can rapidly transform those individual gut feelings into a collective and unified organisational perspective.

While artificial intelligence may not yet excel at generating unique insights, it can be highly effective at aggregating and interpreting their meaning. Through NLP, AI can convert qualitative, experience-based input into structured data. It can then compare these data points across various contributors, integrating them with its existing knowledge base to formulate a cohesive organisational perspective. This perspective is refined through an iterative cycle, allowing the system to evolve toward a broadly accepted view that reflects collective intelligence.

For example, consider a consulting firm working on a digital transformation strategy for a client. Individual consultants contribute insights based on their sector knowledge, client interactions, and market experience. AI tools equipped with NLP capture these qualitative inputs. These are then structured into comparable data sets. The AI identifies patterns and integrates this with external data. Over several iterations, the firm arrives at a well-rounded strategic recommendation which reflects both the nuance of individual expertise and the coherence of collective intelligence.

Creating Knowledge Cycles

The biggest value driver of AI solutions is that, unlike traditional systems, they are not static but learn and grow as more data is fed into them. This means that, once insights are codified into structured data, intelligence can be generated that may be used by the agent in other applied situations to assist organisations make better decisions or take more effective action.

However, the uniqueness of the relationship between the artificial and the natural does not stop there. As the AI agent learns, it builds new intelligence which is either communicated or transferred to humans in a digestible format, subsequently adding new data points for human insights, which can in turn be translated into intelligence... In this way, a knowledge cycle is created where learning and knowledge transfer never stops.

Once again, however, this comes with a word of caution. Although artificial and human intelligence can learn from each other, the processing capability of humans is biologically constrained and can never match the power and speed of AI. Theoretically speaking, since machines learn at a faster rate than humans, there will come a point where our intelligence becomes outmatched, and that could spell our doom.

Heartfulness – Connecting Stakeholders to a Common Purpose

Despite their growing capabilities, machines lack emotions. Unlike humans, machines cannot empathise, laugh, cry, or find joy in the company of others. Their functioning is rooted solely in logic and reasoning. While some advanced agents can mimic emotional responses, these are mere simulations. They do not possess genuine feelings and, as a result, cannot form the deep emotional bonds or authentic connections that arise naturally between people.

In a world built by humans for humans, this is a fatal business limitation, since customers place the greatest value on the emotions a purchase generates. Despite all the incredible developments in technology, to date there is no better way of creating positive emotions than a relationship between one human and another. (Although, being an avid fan of the Big Bang Theory, I smile at the thought of Raj (incapable of speaking to women) developing a seemingly romantic relationship with Siri!)

Whilst emotional bonds between humans and machines will hopefully not become a widespread thing, there is definitely a case for using artificial intelligence to enhance the emotional responses and experiences of humans. For instance, machine learning can help us to better understand individualised customer preferences, leading to the development of more personalised services. On the other hand, augmented reality and/or virtual reality, when combined with AI, can enhance the experience of the customer through the stimulation of other senses of the body.

Balancing Intelligence with Insight and Heartfulness

Although Artificial Intelligence is transforming the way professionals work, its real power emerges when it is combined with human insight. As we have seen, intelligence is not just about data and speed, but about applying experience, emotion, and purpose to guide decisions.

The HumAInity Works framework encourages us to treat AI as a co-pilot rather than a replacement for our judgements, actions and decisions. Firms that strike this balance will not only adapt to change but lead it, thereby delivering smarter outcomes while staying grounded in what matters most.

About David Galea

David Galea is the founder of HumAInity Works, a venture dedicated to helping professional service firms thrive in a rapidly evolving digital economy. With over twenty-five years of experience in strategic transformation, David specialises in blending artificial intelligence with human insight to drive innovation, sustainable growth, and competitive advantage. He has worked extensively across accountancy, legal, consulting, and technology sectors, developing practical AI maturity models and frameworks tailored to the unique dynamics of knowledge-based businesses.

David is the author of Digital Made Simple, which won a Bronze Medal at the prestigious Axiom Business Book Awards. His work has been instrumental in enabling firms to embrace digital change while preserving their core human values. In addition to his advisory work, David is a respected speaker, mentor, and podcast host, committed to exploring how AI can be used ethically and effectively to elevate the role of professionals in society.

AI as the Great Equaliser: Challenging Our Existing Paradigms

ERIK SCHWARTZ

Sam Altman stared at his laptop screen in the pre-dawn darkness of November 30, 2022. The offices of OpenAI in San Francisco's Mission District were nearly empty, save for a handful of engineers monitoring server loads. Outside, the city slept, unaware that everything was about to change.

They had decided to launch quietly – no fanfare, no press release, just a tweet and a blog post: "today we launched ChatGPT. try talking with it here: chat.openai.com".

Altman's finger hovered over the enter key. Three years of work. Billions in investment. Careers on the line. He clicked.

What happened next would shatter every record in consumer technology history.

Within five days, a million users had signed up. The servers groaned and crashed, then crashed again. Engineers worked around the clock, adding capacity as fast as they could. By January, ChatGPT had amassed 100 million users, reaching that milestone faster than any other consumer application before it. The telegraph took seventy-five years to reach fifty million users. The telephone took fifty years. ChatGPT needed just two months to double that number.

But this wasn't merely about breaking records. Something more profound was unfolding. In a cramped apartment in Lagos, a young entrepreneur named Adaora Okafor stayed up until dawn, tears streaming down her face as ChatGPT helped her write a business plan in polished English. "For the first time," she would later say, "I felt like I could compete with anyone in the world."

In rural Kansas, sixteen-year-old Marcus Chen stared at his calculus homework at 3AM. His underfunded school had no tutoring program. His parents, immigrants who worked double shifts, had neither the time nor the education to help him. In desperation, he typed his problem into ChatGPT. Within seconds the AI had solved the equations, and within minutes it had walked him through each step so that he could do so himself. "It was like having Einstein as my personal tutor," he said.

In Mumbai, at 2AM, marketing manager Priya Sharma sat back in her chair, stunned. "It's like having a brilliant intern who never gets tired, never needs coffee, and knows everything about everything," she told her husband, who thought she was hallucinating from exhaustion.

The convergence had arrived. A technology had stopped being a tool and started becoming a partner.

The History of Transformation

The morning of January 15, 1880, Thomas Edison sat in his Menlo Park laboratory, surrounded by failure. He had tested over 3,000 materials for his incandescent light bulb. His hands were burned, his eyes bloodshot, and his room was still lit by gas lamps. "Genius," he would later say, "is one percent inspiration and ninety-nine percent perspiration."

When the bulb finally glowed steady and bright, Edison couldn't have known his invention would illuminate more than just rooms. It would illuminate a path toward a future where human ingenuity could be amplified beyond recognition.

But the real acceleration came on a freezing December morning in 1903. Orville Wright lay prone on a contraption that looked more like a death trap than the future. The wind at Kitty Hawk cut through his clothes like knives. His brother, Wilbur, ran alongside, shouting encouragement over the roar of the engine.

Twelve seconds. 120 feet. In that brief moment, humanity slipped the bonds of Earth.

Within a single human lifetime, just sixty-six years later, Neil Armstrong would set foot on the moon. A person born in 1900 could have shaken the hand that flew the first airplane and the hand that touched lunar soil. No previous century had witnessed such compression of achievement.

This was the Great Acceleration, the age when humanity's impact on Earth shifted into overdrive. These innovations didn't just change what we could do. They changed who we could become.

The Digital Revolution's Four Waves

By the 1970s, a new revolution was stirring in California garages. Steve Jobs was twenty-one when he and Steve Wozniak sold their first Apple I computer in 1976. Jobs had just returned from India, searching for meaning. Wozniak was a brilliant engineer who thought computers should be fun. Together, they would democratise computing power.

"We didn't know what we didn't know," Jobs would later reflect. While IBM executives in grey suits insisted computers belonged in corporate data centres, two college dropouts were soldering circuit boards in a garage, convinced that the future belonged to everyone.

The second wave arrived when Tim Berners-Lee, a soft-spoken British scientist, faced a problem at CERN. Physicists worldwide couldn't easily share research. His solution was elegantly simple: documents that could link to other documents. "Vague but exciting," his boss wrote on the proposal.

By 1993, there were only 130 websites. By 2000, there were over 17 million. The web had grown faster than any communication medium in history, turning the internet from a network of computers into a network of human minds.

The third wave crashed ashore on January 9, 2007. Steve Jobs, now greying but still magnetic, stood at San Francisco's Moscone Center. He reached into his pocket with theatrical precision. "Every once in a while, a revolutionary product comes along that changes everything."

The iPhone wasn't just a phone. It was the internet in your pocket, a camera, a GPS, a thousand tools collapsed into a handheld rectangle of glass and metal. By 2010, there were five billion mobile subscriptions worldwide. Farmers in Kenya were banking on their phones. Protesters in Egypt were organising revolutions via Twitter.

The fourth wave, cloud computing, arrived quietly. Amazon Web Services meant anyone could rent supercomputer power by the hour. A startup in a Bangalore apartment could deploy services that scaled to billions of clients. The playing field hadn't just been levelled; it had been transformed into something new entirely.

Each wave had shortened the adoption cycle. Radio took thirty-eight years to reach fifty million users. Television took thirteen. The internet took four. Facebook took three and a half. But these were gentle swells compared to the tsunami about to hit.

The ChatGPT Phenomenon

Greg Brockman, OpenAI's president, couldn't sleep on November 29, 2022. They had tested ChatGPT extensively, but releasing it to the world was different. "What if it says something horrible?" he worried. "What if no one cares?"

Within hours of launch, his phone exploded with notifications. Twitter was on fire. Users shared conversations where ChatGPT wrote Shakespearean sonnets about pizza, explained quantum physics in the style of a pirate, debugged complex code, and offered relationship advice with the wisdom of a thousand therapists.

The screenshots went viral. Then viral again. Servers crashed under the load. "We thought it would be interesting," Brockman later admitted, laughing at the understatement. "We didn't expect it to break the internet."

Grandmothers were using it to write birthday cards that made their grandchildren cry. CEOs were using it to draft strategic memos that wowed their boards. Priya crafted a marketing plan that would have taken her team a week. Marcus crushed a calculus assignment he would have failed.

The same tool, equally powerful, equally accessible to all.

"We've hit an inflection point," Sam Altman tweeted as user numbers climbed into the stratosphere. What he didn't say, what he perhaps couldn't yet fully grasp, was that this inflection point wasn't just about a successful product. It was about humanity crossing a threshold from which there was no return.

The Knowledge Revolution

Dr Sarah Chen was crying at her desk in Johns Hopkins Hospital at 3AM. The twenty-eight-year-old resident had been on call for twenty-two hours straight. Her patient, a seven-year-old boy named Tyler, was dying, and she didn't know why.

Persistent fever. Strawberry tongue. Bloodshot eyes. Nothing matched. Her attending had shrugged and ordered more tests. But Chen could see it in Tyler's mother's eyes: they were running out of time.

Desperate, she pulled out her phone and opened ChatGPT.

"Consider Kawasaki disease," the AI suggested. "Time is critical. Untreated Kawasaki can lead to coronary artery aneurysms within days."

Chen's hands trembled as she ordered the echocardiogram. The tests confirmed it. Tyler received treatment within hours. Two weeks later, he was playing soccer again.

"In medical school, they taught us when you hear hoofbeats, think horses, not zebras," Chen later reflected. "But sometimes it is a zebra. And now we have something that's memorised every animal in the zoo."

For all of human history, expertise had been scarce. Now, suddenly, everyone had access to the sum of human knowledge, and it could talk back.

The Multiplication of Human Potential

Marcus Thompson had been coding for fifteen years, but the Austin developer was struggling with a problem that had stumped his team for weeks. At 11PM on a Friday, he decided to try ChatGPT.

Four hours later, he had built an entire application that would have taken a month to complete.

"Every friction point just disappeared," he explained to his stunned colleagues. "The AI knew the syntax, could explain approaches, spotted patterns I was missing..."

Thompson's productivity exploded. He was shipping features at ten times his previous rate. "I'm a backend developer, but suddenly I was building beautiful frontends, implementing machine learning. It was like having the collective knowledge of every programmer who ever lived whispering in my ear."

The Great Leveller

Sam Altman leaned forward at the TED conference in April 2024. "We're going to see a one-person billion-dollar company by 2026," he declared. "Maybe sooner."

In Brooklyn, twenty-six-year-old Maya Patel was well on her way. From her one-bedroom apartment, she had built an AI-powered consulting firm that was stealing contracts from McKinsey.

ChatGPT handled research. Claude managed documentation. Midjourney created presentations. GitHub Copilot built custom solutions. Her "team" never slept, never complained, never asked for raises.

"I have the cognitive firepower of a 50-person firm," Maya explained. "Last week, I underbid Accenture by 90% and still made more profit than I ever dreamed possible."

Institutional Disruption

Goldman Sachs sent out a memo in March 2024 that shook Wall Street. They were cutting their analyst program by 60%.

"We don't need armies of junior analysts anymore," admitted one managing director. "One senior banker with AI can do what used to require a whole bullpen."

For Generation Z, the floor had dropped out. The traditional career ladder had its lower rungs sawed off while they were still climbing.

Universities faced an even deeper crisis. When ChatGPT passed the bar exam and aced MBA coursework, the value proposition of a $200,000 education came under assault.

Professor Jennifer Walsh at Harvard watched her lecture hall empty. "Students realised they could ask ChatGPT to explain quantum mechanics better than I could."

The Societal Reckoning

In Davos, January 2025, the usual swagger was gone. In closed-door sessions, CEOs whispered their fears.

"If one person with AI can do the work of a hundred," asked a bank CEO, his voice cracking, "what do the other ninety-nine do?"

The World Economic Forum predicted eighty-three million jobs lost to AI by 2027, offset by only sixty-nine million new ones. A net loss of fourteen million jobs.

"We're facing a crisis of meaning," explained Dr Viktor Andersson. "For centuries, we've defined ourselves by our work. What happens when those identities vanish overnight?"

Navigating the New Paradigm

As 2025 dawned, humanity stood at a crossroads that made previous technological transitions look like gentle curves in the road. This was a cliff, and we were racing toward it at full speed.

Dr Sarah Chen, the resident who'd saved Tyler's life with ChatGPT's help, had become an unlikely voice in the storm. "The technology isn't good or evil," she insisted at conference after conference. "It's a mirror that reflects and amplifies who we are. If we approach it with wisdom and humanity, it will make us wiser and more human. If we approach it with greed and fear, it will make us greedy and fearful."

Maya Patel, now running a $50 million revenue company from a slightly larger apartment in Brooklyn, had discovered something profound. "AI gave me superhuman capabilities," she reflected. "But my clients don't hire me for what the AI can do. They hire me for judgement, for creativity, for understanding what they really need, not just what they ask for. AI is my bicycle, but I still choose where to ride."

In his San Francisco office, Sam Altman opened his laptop to check ChatGPT's statistics. 500 million weekly users. Two billion conversations. Humanity talking to its creation, and the creation talking back.

He began typing a query to GPT-5, still in development: "How do we ensure AI remains humanity's tool rather than its master?"

The cursor blinked, waiting. But even as he waited, Altman knew the answer wouldn't come from the machine. It would come from us.

About Erik Schwartz

Erik Schwartz is a seasoned technology executive and entrepreneur with over two decades of experience in the tech sector, specialising in search and knowledge discovery. As the Fractional CAIO behind aiexpert. ai, Erik has been at the forefront of integrating Large Language Models (LLMs) and Generative AI into search technologies.

His illustrious career includes key senior roles at Comcast, Elsevier, and Microsoft, where he led pioneering AI, search, and LLM initiatives. Erik has firmly established himself as a trusted leader in the technology community. In his role as a virtual chief AI officer, Erik leverages his extensive experience to develop and implement comprehensive AI strategies for small and medium businesses.

The AI Expert: where AI expertise meets real-world application.

🌐 www.theaiexpert.ai

Smarter Machines Need Wiser Humans: How to Stay Human, Trusted, and Valuable in the Age of AI

LEIGH ALLEN

Beware the Simplicity Trap

We're living in a world where speed is sold as progress. Where clicking a button can draft a strategy, write a speech, or make a decision, without much thought behind it. AI has made that possible. And, let's be honest, it's impressive.

But just because something is easy doesn't mean it's right. And just because a machine can do something, doesn't mean we should let it. In fact, the easier something becomes, the more intentional we need to be about why we're doing it, and what we might be giving up. In my work advising organisations through the challenges of complexity, I've learned that ease can sometimes be a trap. It makes us skip the conversation, the reflection, the deliberate pause that gives meaning to a decision. We risk confusing speed with progress, and output with impact.

AI is accelerating everything, but with that speed comes growing complexity: more data, more choices, more pressure to respond instantly. As humans, we must resist the pull toward what I've come to think of as "machine simplicity" – surface-level ease without true understanding. Machines streamline; humans make sense. There's a world of difference between something being easy to do and something being right to do.

In leadership, we're looking for the simplicity that lives on the other side of complexity. The kind that only emerges when you've done the hard work of thinking it through, engaging with others, and facing the difficult questions. Machine simplicity flattens that process. Human simplicity honours it. And it's that kind of simplicity – thoughtful, earned, and grounded – that makes decisions stick and builds lasting trust.

I've worked in high-pressure environments most of my life: military, policing, digital forensics, and now strategic advisory. And what I've learned is this: the best decisions aren't the fastest ones. They're the ones made with care, context, and connection. That's what wisdom looks like in the real world.

AI doesn't offer wisdom. It offers convenience and tends to oversimplify. And while that can be incredibly useful, there's a danger in getting too comfortable with it.

When we start letting machines do our thinking for us, our writing, our problem-solving, even our conversations, we risk something deeper than lost skills. We risk losing the very parts of ourselves that others trust us for: our judgement, our presence, our empathy.

We don't trust someone because they've got all the right answers. We trust them because they care. Because they show up when it's hard. Because they take the time to listen, to reflect, and to choose wisely. Machines don't do that. That's still our job.

And yet I see leaders relying on AI tools to replace their own reflection, their own voice, even their own learning. There's no harm in using AI to help. The problem is when we start to think that's enough.

In my work, I often remind people that trust isn't built by outputs alone. Of course, results matter, but competence is only one part of the equation. Trust is built not just through what we achieve, but through how we show up, especially under pressure. It requires of us something deeper and more human.

I use my ICCE model to frame it:

- Integrity is about doing what you say you will, even when no one is watching.

- Competence is about showing you can deliver.

- Care is the sense that you're genuinely invested in others.

- Empathy is your ability to understand how others feel and respond accordingly.

When all four components of the ICCE model are present, trust grows – trust not only in what you can do, but in who you are. Without care and empathy, there can be no lasting trust; and without lasting trust, people won't follow you for long even if you hit your targets.

AI doesn't carry that kind of weight. It never will. It can assist, inform, and even inspire, but it won't ever care. It won't ever have skin in the game. And deep down, we all know that.

If we're serious about leading in this new era, we need to hold on tightly to the things that make us human, especially when they're inconvenient. Thoughtfulness. Empathy. Conscience. They're slower, messier, and harder to scale. But they're also the things people will still follow you for, even when AI can do the rest.

Double Down on What Makes You Human

To ensure we retain and centre our human qualities, we need practical frameworks. The ICCE model will help you win the trust of your clients, but to really thrive in the age of AI acceleration, you'll need to go further.

That's why I look at my work through a simple but powerful lens: Purpose, Clarity, and Trust.

- Purpose keeps you anchored in why the work matters.

- Clarity helps you work through the complexity and act with intent.

- Trust creates the space for people to speak up, lean in, and move forward together.

Look at any recent decision you had with AI, or any discussion with a human that was informed by AI. Did you stop and ask, "Is this the right thing?" Or was it just the easy thing? Audit your week. Where have convenience and oversimplification crept in where care and consideration might have served you better?

We don't need to keep up with machines. We need to become more of what they're not.

If you're feeling the pressure to do more, decide faster, or keep pace with tech, you're not alone. But speed and volume were never the measure of great leadership.

Depth, discernment, and emotional clarity were. And they still are.

That's why I talk about building your CORE, the four human strengths that keep you grounded, trusted, and valuable in a world of automation. They are:

- Cognition – thinking clearly and critically.

- Originality – creating meaningfully and uniquely.

- Relational intelligence – building trust and emotional presence.

- Ethics – doing the right thing, not just the efficient thing.

These aren't abstract qualities. They're the difference between being followed and being forgotten.

Let's break them down.

Cognition – Think Beyond the Algorithm

AI can synthesise and summarise, but it can't make meaning the way we can. It doesn't reflect on complexity, challenge assumptions, or weigh long-term consequences. It tends towards "machine simplicity".

Real thinking requires space. It demands discipline. It takes courage to slow down when everything around you is speeding up.

Before acting on an AI insight, pause and ask, "If this wasn't handed to me, what would I have noticed instead?" Follow this with "Does this feel complete, or simply convenient?"

Originality – Say Something That Matters

AI can remix the past. It can't create from lived experience.

But you can.

The most powerful insights come from curiosity, intuition, and lived reflection, not algorithms. Your originality is your signal. It's how you cut through the noise. In a world full of noise, meaning stands out.

Try keeping a "human signals" notebook. Capture the small things – a moment of clarity, a reaction, a shift in tone. Feed those into your work. That's the raw material AI can't replicate.

Relational Intelligence – The Trust Multiplier

We don't build momentum through process alone. We build it through trust. And trust is what gives people the courage to show up fully, speak their mind, and challenge the status quo. That's psychological safety in action, and without it, you will never achieve deep insights, build deep processes or forge deep bonds.

Don't delegate care. Where in your workflow does someone need a moment of human presence, not just an automated message?

Ethics – Carry the Weight Machines Can't

This is where it all comes together.

AI doesn't carry values. It doesn't know if something is just, inclusive, or harmful. That responsibility is ours.

Apply the CORE method when considering key decisions:

- Cognition: have I thought this through with clarity?

- Originality: am I adding anything uniquely human?

- Relational intelligence: Who is affected, and have I considered them fully?

- Ethics: is this the right thing, not just the fastest thing?

These aren't soft skills. They're hard-won strengths, the kind people will still pay for, still follow, and still remember.

And purpose, clarity, and trust are at the heart of them. Purpose connects to your originality and ethical stance. Clarity sharpens your cognition. And trust, of course, lives in your relationships. When these elements are present, they create the psychological safety people need to experiment, challenge ideas, and contribute fully.

Be the Human Others Can Trust

Let's put this myth to rest: AI won't replace human judgement. But it will test it, every single day.

If anything, judgement will matter more in an AI world, not less. Because now, you're not just deciding what to do, you're deciding what to trust, what to delegate, and what to stand for.

And that's where many people get caught out. They treat AI like a faster brain, when it's just a powerful assistant. Helpful? Absolutely. But it doesn't hold any responsibility. You do.

Responsibility is about judgement, and in turn, judgement is about being deliberate – about weighing context, intent, and consequence. Machines can't do this, because they can't feel the weight of a decision. But good leaders do, and that's exactly what makes them trustworthy.

In practical terms, judgement means slowing down just enough to ask:

- Does this make sense in the real world, or just on paper?

- Who's affected if I get this wrong?

- What's missing that a machine might not see?

Judgement is also about pattern-breaking. AI is trained on what was. But leadership is often about doing what hasn't been done yet. That takes courage, not computation. And it starts by being willing to say, "This doesn't feel right," even when the data says otherwise.

In every decision worth making, there's a moment when you feel the tension between speed and depth, between clarity and complexity. That's your signal. It's the part of the process you shouldn't rush, because it's where your wisdom lives.

The best leaders I've worked with over the years have one thing in common: they don't just act fast; they act well. They bring others into the decision. They listen for what's not being said. They hold the silence when it would be easier to fill it. They work through the complexity.

That's judgement in action.

Here's something we don't say enough: AI is just infrastructure. It's the new electricity, or the new internet. We're still talking about it like it's the thing. But soon, we won't say "I used AI," any more than we say, "I used the internet."

What will matter is how we apply it. What apps we use. How we design workflows, conversations, and decisions around it. The winners in this space won't be the ones shouting about AI; they'll be the ones quietly making it work, in ways that enhance humans, for human reasons.

So don't outsource your judgement. Strengthen it. Protect it. Practise it. Let purpose anchor it. Let clarity sharpen it. Let trust flow from it. Judgement isn't a soft skill. It's a survival skill. And it's going to be more valuable than ever.

In the age of AI, the temptation is to trust the output more than your own instinct. But when things go wrong, when the stakes are high or the data is incomplete, people won't be looking for a tool. They'll be looking for someone who can hold the weight of uncertainty and still move forward with care.

Be the human others can trust. Your values, your judgement, and your vision are what set you apart.

About Leigh Allen

Leigh is a trusted strategic advisor, leadership coach, and technologist who helps leaders navigate complex digital transformations with purpose, clarity and trust.

His career in public safety spans the army, the police, and the National Crime Agency, where he held senior roles protecting the public and leading complex digital operations. Now as a strategic advisor, Leigh uses his experience and abilities to combine deep technical insight with human-centred leadership. He specialises in building high-performing teams, improving decision-making under pressure, and creating the psychological safety needed for growth and innovation.

Driven by a lifelong mission to help people stay safe and unlock their full potential, Leigh draws on decades of frontline and boardroom experience to challenge assumptions and shift thinking.

Married with four children, he lives in a quiet village in South Leicestershire, where he reflects, writes, and helps others build momentum in a complex world.

AI Will Never Be Able to Take Over Human Creativity

ONUR IBRAHIM

Creativity in Humans

Creativity is not simply a skill we develop. It is part of our very fabric, an intricate thread woven through every human story. From the moment our ancestors painted on cave walls or crafted haunting melodies around fires, creativity has connected us. It's a language of the soul, telling tales of our joys, struggles, fears, and hopes.

To imagine handing this sacred gift over to artificial intelligence feels almost sinful. At its best, AI can replicate patterns and churn out endless variations. But it will never truly understand the reasons behind our creations. Our creativity stems from lived experience. It is born of moments that cut us, heal us, and ultimately shape who we are. That is something no algorithm can genuinely imitate.

AI lacks lived experience, as evident in the many soulless examples of art generated by AI. These creations can trigger synapses, but they lack something special. We are reminded that AI is merely mimicking, creating copies of a copy. Each time, something is lost, eroding the sensibility of the original art. Without human toil, AI-generated art is devoid of depth and emotion and soul. It tries to be too perfect. Many great artists and designers seek perfect imperfection; AI seeks perfect replication of human creation.

Art and creativity are about connection. Connection to each other – to each other through the art, and to the art through each other. Asking systems to create connections when they have never been hurt, loved, failed, or felt a sense of connection is fundamentally flawed.

AI doesn't know how to feel, so how can it create something that evokes genuine emotion? There's a gap. Something significant is missing.

AI Is Speed, Humans Are Depth

We live in an era obsessed with speed. AI fits perfectly into that narrative. It can create volumes of content in seconds, churning out countless articles, stories, or designs. For businesses under pressure to keep feeding the content machine, this is a seductive promise.

But there's a catch.

While AI accelerates production, it doesn't deepen it. AI can provide you with more words faster, but it cannot infuse them with hard-earned insight or genuine soul.

Only humans can transform lines on a page into something that moves hearts and shifts perspectives. We slow down. We reflect. We bleed into our art, leaving parts of ourselves within it. That's what makes creativity worth cherishing.

AI may generate a vast number of words, but only humans can provide the wisdom that truly enriches creativity. We must remember that AI is only predicting one word at a time. The human brain designs and plans an intricate tapestry before a single line is set.

At its core, creativity is about connection. When we write, paint, sing, or dance, we reach out, hoping someone else might understand. Art bridges the gap between our inner world and the world outside. It says, "I've felt this too. You're not alone."

Expecting AI to create meaningful connections is fundamentally flawed. How can something that has never felt pain produce a story that consoles the broken-hearted? How can an entity that has never loved or lost compose a song that brings tears to our eyes? There's simply a void where emotional truth should be.

That void is particularly glaring in writing. AI can generate paragraphs with perfect grammar and a wide vocabulary. Yet it's like a beautifully iced cake that collapses when cut; the substance is missing. True resonance requires more than words on a page. It needs memory, scars, and the wisdom that only humans carry.

Stop the Blank Page from Winning

With all that said, as an augmentation to our creativity, AI can help us create wonderful things. When combined with the human touch, AI eliminates a lot of grunt work, assists with research, and accelerates our writing process. It helps us generate first drafts much faster than we could without it. It automates mundane and repetitive tasks. Think of how many people have sat staring at a blank page, wondering what to write next. AI can help overcome writer's block, preventing the blank page from winning.

Using AI facilitates rapid ideation and enables us to explore new avenues before undertaking research. It can quickly help us explore different frameworks, patterns, and ideas. It provides not just first drafts but fresh starts, collections of random ideas that we can pick and choose from to create something more human and extraordinary.

The Bridge Only Humans Can Build

Art and creativity, at their deepest, are bridge-building. They bridge us to each other and ourselves. We crave connection, and through art and creativity, we can find it. Real resonance is not achieved through clever phrases or trendy pictures. Real resonance is achieved by the plain print of a real life lived.

Consider handing over this sacred task to machinery. The delicate strands that connect us to each other would be lost. The poems and lyrics scribbled in a notepad lying on a single bed in a dingy spare room. The songs born out of agony and wanting. The paintings speaking truths too raw to verbalise. The stories raging against the world. They would all be unheard.

Human imagination is how we navigate grief, honour love, grumble about injustice, and envision better futures. Without it, we would lose much of the richness, the meaning in our lives. And that's why we must struggle to preserve our creative souls. To pass them lock, stock, and barrel to AI would be to erase the very heartbeat that drives us forward.

Your Unwavering Creative Companion

Consider AI as your unwavering creative companion – an asset, an assistant, and an assisted consciousness that supports you in generating more ideas. It can help you negotiate paths that would otherwise take a long time to explore. Think of it as a brainstorming buddy or a blank canvas for thought-provoking conversations.

Protecting the Human Spark

The real secret to living with AI is knowing just where it belongs and where it doesn't. Embrace it as an asset and treat it as a tool, but never use it as a replacement for real human thought and emotions. Let it handle the drudgery that drains your energy. Let it sort out your research, vomit out drafts, and add new ideas to the pot. But always preserve the ultimate act of creation for yourself.

Because it's your opinion, your smile, your pain, and your private victories that give your life meaning. These are riches AI can never compete with. They give your words and your art a pulse that no machine code can ever compete with.

Putting in the Toil

Human imagination is not replaceable; it cannot be outsourced. It's at the very heart of who we are, formed from our personal experiences and woven of a rich fabric of our memories, emotions, and hard-won lessons.

AI lacks the richness of lived experience. It has never felt heartbreak or the spark of excitement. AI creates simulations, copies of copies of copies of emotions. With each layer, fidelity is lost. The physicality of the original fades away, leaving only a fragile mould around a hollow space.

Without human intention guiding it, AI's creations are devoid of soul, motionless.

They may be pleasing to the eye or grammatically perfect on the page. Yet they lack the profound richness and connection that mark true art. Even children sense it. Ask a child which story feels real, and they'll point to the human one. Human authenticity resonates deeply, even with young hearts.

AI Must Remain the Helper, Never the Heartbeat

So let AI be a loyal companion, an ever-present helper, a diligent researcher, and even a sounding board. Utilise the machine to generate more ideas, connect with a broader audience, and discover new opportunities. Let it clean up the clutter so you can focus on building the masterpiece.

But while AI is limitless in its optimism and efficiency, it is also limited. It simply can't replicate the Yin and the Yang that give us balance and truth. Without emotion, without balance, without experience, all stories reduce to flat, dead surfaces.

Keeping the Human Spark at the Centre

So, collaborate with AI. Have it lift the drudgery from you and shower you with ideas. But guard dearly what is most valuable: your voice, your intuition, your battle-won experience. Those are things no machine can ever possess.

Because your beautiful, battered, beating heart cannot be replicated by AI. Only your experiences, fears, triumphs, and hopes can guide the machine. That's the true magic.

So keep writing. Keep painting. Keep singing. Use AI to help you go further and travel faster, but always ensure that it is the human experience that brings it to a final flourish. In an era that is hurtling towards automation, our human imagination is more precious and potent than ever. Stay connected to each other through imagination and creativity. Share your stories with love.

About Onur Ibrahim

From washing dishes in his family's restaurant as a boy, to building and selling agencies. Onur's story is all about keeping the human touch at the heart of it all.

From the late 1990s, Onur has helped everyone from corner pharmacies to global tech to scale with soul. His message is that creativity isn't optional; it's how we connect, grow, and stand out.

Whether he's teaching how to sell with integrity, creating ads that speak to people, building an audience who actually relate to you, or getting AI to help you perform the magic, Onur delivers with enthusiasm, humour, and authenticity. You can expect fresh thinking, challenging of convention, much laughter, and actionable takeaways that will help you build a business people really care about.

🌐 www.onuribrahim.com

🌐 www.commino.co.uk

Perfect Imperfection: Staying Human in the Age of AI

PAUL CAMERON

"To thrive in a world of ever more perfect machines, we must learn to prize the raw, the unfinished, and the brilliantly imperfect qualities of being human. The groove, the instinct, and the presence that no algorithm can replicate."

The Art of the Groove – How Imperfection Creates Connection

Imagine turning up to a Rolling Stones gig and finding five bass players lined up, each playing perfectly tuned, flawlessly executed notes. You'd probably admire their skill for about ten minutes, then feel something hollow. You came to dance, to feel the raw, scuffed-up energy that only the Stones can summon, a sound that's ragged around the edges and much richer for it.

When Keith Richards hits a chord slightly late, or when Jagger's voice cracks in the chorus, that's not a failure of discipline. It's the reason people keep filling stadiums decade after decade. The music feels alive because of it. The groove is imperfect on purpose.

Perfection is surprisingly easy these days. Type a prompt into an AI model, and you'll get exactly what you asked for: a symmetrical logo, a slick proposal, a photo with no stray shadows. But perfection isn't the same as resonance. Perfection doesn't always move people. It doesn't pull them into your world or make them feel seen.

In my work designing treehouses and rope bridges worldwide, I see this all the time. A perfect CAD drawing can't convey the feeling of a child's gasp when they first step onto a swaying rope bridge. A proposal with flawless formatting won't guarantee trust or loyalty. The most enduring work has something of the Rolling Stones in it – slightly out of time, a little raw, but unmistakably alive.

This isn't just a romantic idea. It's a practical one. In a world where machines can produce polished output on demand, what makes you distinctive is your willingness to stay human. To embrace the groove rather than the grid.

I think about when I first started learning the drums. My teacher gave me a neat exercise book full of perfect rudiments, but no matter how accurately I played them, it all sounded lifeless until I began to feel the space between the beats. That moment, when the groove replaced the grid, changed the way I approached every creative endeavour since. Whether you're playing music, building a treehouse, or shaping a conversation, it's the human element – the slight sway or swagger, the pause, the unscripted grin – that brings something to life.

It's the same reason live music feels different from a recording. It's the same reason a hand-drawn sketch has more warmth than a digital render. Perfection can be admired, but imperfection invites us in. It lets us participate.

If you're looking for ways to practice perfect imperfection in your own work, start here:

- Leave space for error. Sometimes, a rough first draft holds the seed of the most interesting ideas.

- Prioritise presence over polish. If you have to choose between being perfectly prepared or fully present, choose presence every time.

- Remember the audience. People don't connect with immaculate execution. They connect with intention and energy.

If the Rolling Stones have taught us anything, it's that the groove matters more than precision. Their success – five decades of sold-out tours and iconic recordings – proves that when you play imperfectly with conviction, you create something that AI cannot: a human experience people want to join in.

In your career, your relationships, and your leadership, the same principle holds. Perfection is cheap now. Groove is priceless. You might spend hours polishing a proposal or refining an algorithm, but it's often the small, unplanned moment – the comment that wasn't rehearsed, the idea you almost didn't share – that makes the lasting impact.

The Upbeat

Before the first note of a symphony, there's a moment that holds everything. The conductor's arms lift, and in that split-second of silence, every musician is watching. The upbeat isn't just a signal to start. It contains the entire spirit of what's about to unfold. A sharp flick of the baton means urgency. A sweeping gesture promises lyricism. A subtle tilt of the head signals something playful.

That single motion is where the music begins in the hearts and minds of the players. The downbeat brings sound, but the upbeat brings intention.

AI is incredibly good at the downbeat, executing instructions. Give it data and a prompt, and it will churn out results with the consistency of a metronome.

But AI can't deliver the intention of the upbeat. It can't communicate purpose, mood, or shared emotional context. Those are human gifts. That's why leadership is not just about telling people what to do. It's about shaping the energy before any action begins.

As a business owner, I've seen this distinction play out countless times. You can automate scheduling, document preparation, even early design drafts. But you can't automate the moment when you look a client in the eye and help them feel understood. You can't delegate the spark that makes a team member feel their contribution matters. You can't script a genuine laugh or the shared excitement of an idea taking shape.

A prompt may generate content, but only a human can generate connection.

I often think about Freddie Mercury at Live Aid, standing alone at the piano in front of 100,000 people. Queen weren't the headliners. They didn't have a new album to sell. But in those first notes, Freddie sent a signal that transformed that global audience into something electric. He lifted the crowd into a shared groove that no machine could orchestrate. It wasn't the precision of his voice that moved people. It was the intention behind it – the invitation to belong, to feel something bigger.

Freddie didn't need a script or an algorithm. He needed to be fully alive to that moment, reading the energy, shaping it, passionately inviting everyone to join. That's the power of the upbeat. The power to set a tone before anything else happens.

In leadership, that power is yours. You are the conductor who can lift a room with a glance or a question. You are the robin who dares to sing a note that no one quite expects. You are the one who can decide whether the day begins in tension or in trust.

In this AI age, leadership won't be measured by who has the smartest software. It will be measured by who can still offer the invisible signal that makes people want to play along.

If you want to lead with an upbeat, not just a downbeat, consider this:

Signal purpose before action. When introducing new technology or change, communicate why it matters.

Set the emotional tone. Whether in a meeting or an email, decide the feeling you want to create.

Invite alignment. The best leaders don't dictate. They invite people to breathe in together before playing the first note.

The more I've worked with teams, the clearer this becomes: the energy you bring to the room will echo long after the meeting ends. The intention you set will shape not only the task at hand but the culture you build. AI can provide the rhythm. Only you can provide the reason.

Playing the Wrong Way, Brilliantly

Consider Jimi Hendrix. He didn't just play the guitar - he reinvented it. Playing left-handed on a right-handed guitar strung for right-handers, everything he played was reversed and inverted. He didn't just play differently. He saw the instrument differently.

He taught himself by listening, by feeling, by trusting that if it sounded good, it was good. He played the wrong way, but he played it so brilliantly that it became the right way – his way.

Today, business and life often come with manuals. Frameworks, best practices, playbooks. Now AI brings us another layer of highly optimised "right answers". Feed it a question, and it will produce the consensus view, the aggregated pattern of what's been done before.

But the consensus view is rarely where genius lives. Genius lives in the upside-down, back-to-front, wrong-way-round approach that feels true even if it doesn't look correct. Hendrix didn't set out to be unconventional for the sake of it. He simply followed his ears.

That's where originality comes from. When you see a project differently, trust your instinct before you trust the manual. The AI can help you explore options, but the final choice should be yours. Even if others don't understand it yet.

I remember the first time I built a treehouse that didn't follow any standard plan. It had odd angles and a walkway that wound around a stand of trees like a curious fox following its own trail. Everyone thought it would look ridiculous or prove impossible to build. But when the family stepped inside, their faces lit up in a way I'll never forget. In that moment, I knew that no spreadsheet could have led me there. No automated model would have suggested such an eccentric design. That was the reward for trusting a belief.

Here are some ways to practice Hendrix thinking:

- Test your instincts. Before asking AI to solve it, spend five minutes sketching your own approach.

- Defy the template. If every solution looks the same, ask yourself what's missing.

- Follow your curiosity. Sometimes the "wrong" method leads to the right breakthrough.

Just like a drummer who loops back to page one of the practice book, mastering not just the notes but the feel, we have to return to our own instincts again and again. Relearning them. Trusting them. Performing them. Because the truth is your best work often emerges when you risk looking foolish.

That's how you move from knowledge to excellence, from practice to performance.

The more perfect the machines become, the more imperfect we must be. Not sloppy or careless, but alive – full of groove, intention, and instinct.

Think of the Rolling Stones' ragged chords, the conductor's poised arms, Hendrix's inverted guitar, or the robin singing a note just because it feels good. They all point to the same truth: what's human is what connects us. What's imperfect is what moves us.

As you build your work and your life alongside AI, remember: your groove, your signal, your upside-down way of seeing the world – that's your greatest asset.

No algorithm can replicate it. No prompt can summon it on demand.

That's the art, and the opportunity, of perfect imperfection.

About Paul Cameron

Paul's lifelong ambition has been to become wonderfully eccentric by retirement – and he's well on his way. A former session drummer turned entrepreneur, he designs and builds treehouses, rope bridges and treetop walkways worldwide, a role often called "the best job in the world".

After studying at the Royal College of Music and serving as professor of music at the Royal Military and Royal Marines Schools of Music, Paul enjoyed a distinguished career. He performed with the London Symphony Orchestra, Royal Opera House and Royal National Theatre, and played on the Oscar-winning film Shakespeare in Love. He also produced acclaimed collaborations, co-produced a Warner Classics top five album, and authored books published by Faber.

Combining his natural business flair with an MBA and creative spirit, Paul founded a company, Treehouse Life Ltd., that transforms childhood dreams into reality. Today, he counts Elton John, Gary Barlow and clients worldwide among his supporters.

Don't Do What You've Always Done

PETER STANSBURY

I started working with computers in the early 1980s, so I've lived through many twists, turns, "transformations" and improvements. I am an eternal optimist, but I tend to dismiss a lot of hype that surrounds everything new. But AI is different. I genuinely believe that AI is a bigger shift than I have ever before seen in my long career.

All my experience suggests that if you simply mix a little AI into your existing ways of working, you'll capture perhaps 10% of the available benefits. But others who explore the true possibilities will make a ten-fold leap in productivity. My advice for living with AI is to be prepared to do things very differently; don't just tweak what you've always done.

There is a natural resistance to change that hinders the adoption of anything new. But the nature of the objections varies according to the change in question. With AI I hear things like: "It's cheating." "It's not authentic." "It's lazy." "People will notice and judge me."

These questions have a place but they are largely misguided.

I'm reminded of a comment made by a highly successful author, many decades ago, who insisted that "real writers" should never use typewriters. "If God meant you to use a typewriter," they said with complete conviction, "he would have given you a keyboard instead of fingers."

For a moment, I believed them. Then logic kicked in. If God had intended us to write with ink on paper, wouldn't our fingernails be nibs with ink flowing from them? I understand this author's personal desire to keep writing with pen and paper, for any number of good reasons, but such an approach isn't something divinely ordained. It's just a personal preference. It's also a preference that comes at a cost.

This pattern repeats itself constantly. The established voices claim new tools are somehow inferior or inauthentic. They try to defend the status quo. But the risk is that those who embrace the change revolutionise their lives while others are held back from realising major benefits.

The Difference between Drift and Shift

Earlier, I described the many "shifts" I have experienced during my career. Evolutionary biologists use the terms "drift" and "shift" to explain differences in how species mutate and change. A drift is a random change somewhere in the DNA of an animal. A creature is born with spots instead of stripes, and this slightly improves their camouflage. But it's not enough to keep the animal hidden from the bigger animals that hunt it. If spots are to become more prevalent than stripes, further evolutions need to occur.

But with AI, we are experiencing a shift – a development that fundamentally answers the pressures of the environment, a transformation so useful, so necessary, that it changes things forever. An animal is born with webbed toes and discovers it can swim twice as fast as its brothers and sisters. Its siblings fall prey to the fish that hunt them, but the anomaly escapes to live another day. In a few generations, every baby of the species is born with webbed toes.

That's evolution: that's what we're going through today.

In the business world, the terms of natural selection are the same as in the animal kingdom. Drift is gradual, little changes that add up over time – this is what I call the 10% (10% improvement). But shift is a big change that shakes everything up – this is what I call the 10x (ten times the improvement).

I once saw this play out with a friend of mine. When I visited his swanky office in Hong Kong, I was impressed by its size and cleanliness, and most of all, by the view! We discussed a project, looking over documents and spreadsheets; they used WordPerfect and Lotus123, cutting edge at the time. Then I realised something.

"Where's your computer?" I asked.

"Oh, I don't have one," he said, like it was the most natural thing in the world. "My secretary has the computer next door."

His entire workflow was this elaborate system: he'd dictate documents; she'd type them up, print them out; he'd handwrite amendments; she'd process them on the computer, reprint them... Everything moved through traditional in-tray, out-tray systems. It worked, but it was incredibly inefficient given the potential of the technology at the secretary's fingertips. My friend had drifted.

The next time I saw him, everything had changed. He and his wife and had started their own legal practice, they'd learned to use computers, mastered WordPerfect, and embraced email and faxes over traditional letters. With no support staff, they were now taking on the world's largest law firms and winning. They'd embraced the shift and achieved 10x results, not just 10% improvements.

This is the AI shift: not making your current processes slightly better but fundamentally reimagining how you work.

Stop Thinking 10%

There were clear personal benefits to using a typewriter: legibility improved dramatically (especially if you have handwriting like mine), and typing was faster than writing by hand if you learned to touch-type (though many didn't). Once you factored in the hassles – buying and changing ribbons, fixing alignment, dealing with mechanical issues, creating tables – you were looking at a 10% improvement over handwriting.

No doubt there were plenty of discussions around the water cooler – or whatever the equivalent was back then! – dismissing all the noise around this new technology as nothing more than hype. After all, 10%'s not nothing, but it's hardly a revolution.

Fortunately, some people saw it differently, and it was these visionaries that ushered in a huge social change. The typewriter essentially created the modern office secretary role and dramatically increased women's participation in the workforce. Before typewriters, most clerical work was done by male clerks with elaborate handwriting. By 1930, about 95% of stenographers and typists were women, who had improved their typing skills, leaving the men behind. This was one of the first major technology-driven shifts in gender roles in the workplace.

Typewriters also enabled the modern corporate office structure. Carbon copies allowed for systematic record-keeping and communication chains. Multiple copies of documents enabled new forms of bureaucracy and management oversight. The standardisation of business correspondence changed how companies communicated internally and externally.

All thanks to the typewriter, and the professionals who saw the potential for a shift.

Don't Ignore the Risks

AI is also going to usher in huge social change, whatever personal choices you make.

Before typewriters, clerical work was a male profession seen as a pathway to business leadership, with male clerks often becoming managers or partners. But when women became associated with typing, the role was redefined as supportive rather than leadership-oriented.

Regressive, certainly – but there's a lesson in that too. The typewriter shows how new technologies can simultaneously create opportunities and reinforce existing power structures. It's a reminder that, with AI, we need to be intentional about who gets to do the "strategic work" versus who just "operates the tools".

So, whilst I encourage you to embrace the change, I would also urge you to play your part in ensuring the benefits of AI are shared equally and widely, and that biases aren't reinforced.

Who Cares If It's Artificial?

The word "artificial" carries unnecessary baggage. We're not talking about fake intelligence; we're talking about a different type of intelligence. And that's where the real value emerges – in the combination of human creativity and AI capability.

Let's address some common objections:

"It's cheating." What does cheating mean in this context? Is it cheating when:

- You use a calculator instead of doing long division by hand?

- You use GPS instead of a paper map?

- You drive instead of walking or riding a horse?

All too often people say "cheating" when they mean "doing it differently" or "doing it in a way I don't understand". When Dick Fosbury changed the way we high jump, eyebrows were raised. But I can't remember when I last saw a high jumper do anything but a "Fosbury Flop".

"It's lazy." This reveals a fundamental misunderstanding of productivity. If lazy means doing nothing when you should be doing something, that's problematic. But if lazy means using less energy to achieve excellent results, then that's not lazy, that's efficient. It's the difference between whipping your horse harder and inventing the car.

"It's not authentic." Authenticity has become a buzzword without clear meaning. When you buy a Mercedes assembled by robots, do you think, "This isn't a Mercedes"? When you read a book, do you demand to know if the author used a pen and paper? Authenticity isn't about the tools used; it's about the intention behind the work, the creativity, and the value.

"What if people notice and judge?" This fear is largely unfounded. I used to write with pen and paper, correcting mistakes by crossing them out; later, I used a typewriter and Tippex (remember that smell?) Now I use a word processor. Has anyone ever judged me for this? No. They judge me on whether my ideas are valuable and whether I communicate them clearly.

The tools you use to create are invisible to the end user. What matters is the value you deliver.

Forget the Flag Man

Here's a piece of history: when cars were first introduced, both the UK and US required someone carrying a flag to walk in front of each one, alerting pedestrians and horse-drawn vehicles to the approaching danger. This "flag man" regulation perfectly illustrates how we often respond to transformative technology: by limiting it until it's barely more useful than what came before.

A car that can only travel at walking pace offers limited benefits. You won't get tired, you're protected from the elements, you can carry more cargo, but you're missing the real opportunity. The regulations claimed to save lives but were actually stifling progress.

The invention of the car horn helped. Instead of requiring a flag man, drivers could simply honk to announce their presence.

Today's AI sceptics are essentially demanding their own flag man. They want extensive disclaimers, complicated approval processes, and artificial limitations that prevent AI from delivering its full value. While some caution is warranted, we can't let fear paralyse progress.

The AI Difference - Democratisation

I co-run a small consultancy. When I first founded the company, there were some areas where we could never dream of competing with the big players. With their army of graduates, and staff around the world, they could turn around reports at a pace we simply couldn't match. But with AI we can get work done in hours that would have previously taken days if not weeks. Never mind the hiring costs for support staff.

However, one of the most exciting opportunities I'm seeing with AI is "democratisation". I've worked with schools here and abroad, and I've found that teachers everywhere (including my wife) are overloaded with tasks.

The result is that private schools, with their small class sizes and bigger budgets, have an edge. But now AI is blunting that edge and democratising education. Routine admin can be automated, communications with parents drafted, and lesson plans customised for varying abilities – freeing up teachers to teach.

I'm also seeing great leaps forward in healthcare, from the transcription of meeting notes into medically compliant records through to diagnostic support. The pairing of AI and human intelligence is particularly powerful in the healthcare environment, where systems-thinking and person-centric care interact so dynamically. Progress is especially striking in developing countries, whereas it used to be the preserve of rich countries.

And health isn't only becoming democratised in a clinical setting. In my spare time, I'm a track and field coach. Personalised profiling and training plans used to be the preserve of the professionals with full time coaches. Now anyone can produce them, democratising performance.

The Four Day Week

Yet despite all this change and productivity improvements a problem remains, as summarised by Juliet Schor: "We've been stuck at a five-day week, and the gains from productivity improvements have either been lost to Parkinson's Law [work expands to fill the available time] or funnelled into the pockets of owners."

What if we can make it different this time? Imagine a world where you get five days of work done in four. This only requires a 20% saving. Looking at the capabilities of AI, not only in the present but in the future, does this seem so out of reach?

The Path Forward

Success in the AI era requires a fundamental mindset shift. Stop asking whether you should use AI and start asking how you can use it most effectively. Stop thinking about modest improvements and start imagining transformational possibilities.

The people who will thrive are those who recognise this moment for what it is: not just another drift or technological upgrade, but a major shift, reimagining what's possible. They'll be the ones who abandon their old playbooks, embrace new tools, and create value in ways that were impossible just months ago.

We must not abandon our responsibilities to society. AI will undoubtedly bring in significant social change and there are risks and ethical concerns. But if we do not drive this change ourselves, then such decisions will be made for us.

The choice is yours. You can stick with familiar methods and achieve familiar results, or you can step into the unknown and discover what you're truly capable of achieving.

About Peter Stansbury

Peter has been at the forefront of transformational change from the early days of personal computing through to today's AI revolution. His career spans sales, marketing and leadership roles at innovative tech startups and prestigious advisory firms like Gartner. Today he helps organisations navigate disruptive technologies and unlock exponential growth opportunities.

Peter has guided many companies through the process of technology adoption, witnessing firsthand how organisations that embrace fundamental change, rather than incremental improvements, achieve breakthrough results while their competitors struggle to keep pace.

Peter lives in Buckinghamshire with his wife and two children (well, not children anymore). He makes the most of the time he has saved with AI at the athletics track, coaching, running, jumping and throwing things.

in www.linkedin.com/in/peterstansbury/

✉ peter@stansburys.co.uk

Living a Plan, Leveraging AI

TIM MEADOWS-SMITH

These days, I'm feeling more relaxed than at any other time in a long and richly rewarding career. All this while achieving more than I ever thought possible, thanks to the power of AI.

Of course, it isn't just me. There's not just a charge in the air, there's a revolution. Artificial intelligence, now long embedded in the infrastructure of big corporations, has finally broken free into everyday use. The electricity it generates is beginning to flow through the veins of smaller businesses, public bodies, and ordinary individuals. It is rapidly changing everything: the way we do things, how we are employed, and our entire social structure. It might be daunting, but it's also a thrilling opportunity.

I've always believed in the power of continuous learning, but never has it been more necessary or more rewarding. The AI tools now at our disposal represent a turning point. There is an imperative to learn how to use them properly, and to our collective advantage. These tools are far from a shortcut for the lazy. AI will not do the thinking for you; it cannot replace expertise, only magnify its impact. It offers massive rewards for those who know how to think. For me, that has been the great revelation: productivity improves most dramatically when you combine these tools with genuine, grounded knowledge.

For the past decade, I've been helping business owners scale their operations through a process I call Enterprisation. In essence, Enterprisation moves a business from founder-led improvisation to something more structured, disciplined, and ultimately liberating. It's not about turning entrepreneurs into bureaucrats. Quite the opposite. It's about giving them back their time, their focus and, very often, their joy. When a business begins to run on rhythm and rigour rather than memory and mood, everything changes. The thoughtful application of AI allows us to accelerate that shift dramatically – and with a lot less effort and cost.

What I've come to understand is that AI is a multiplier. If you are already an expert in your field, it enables you to operate at far greater speed and scale. If you try to fake it, then expect it to make you look almost competent for a short while until, quite suddenly, it doesn't. The danger with using a tool that learns from you is that you come to assume the tool knows better than you. It doesn't. It was never designed to. You are the master of the tool, but only if you know how. The outputs are only as good as the inputs, and the inputs are only as good as the thinking that shapes them.

The work I do with business leaders is grounded in a very simple principle: success is built on a plan. Not a plan that sits in a drawer, but one that is lived. A plan that guides decisions, that's reviewed regularly, measured, revised, and improved. This is the beating heart of productivity, and the great corporations have been perfecting it for more than a century. It just so happens that AI is particularly effective at supporting that process, from structure and analysis to automation and review.

Used effectively, AI reduces the wasted energy that so often drains leaders. It can transform businesses – not because of the technology itself, but through how it allows leaders to finally commit to the idea of leading through a repeatable rhythm, supported by the right tools.

It is this very commitment to structure, and the processes that support it, that creates the space to achieve more in less time and, accordingly, the opportunity to reclaim joy. That's not a word we use often enough in business, but it matters. When you have confidence in your direction, and when the machinery of your business hums along without constant intervention, you regain the one thing every founder eventually craves: freedom – peace of mind, the space to think and reflect, and the chance to follow the 80/20 rule determined by Pareto, which recommends you spend your time where it has the most impact.

None of this is about perfection. The current generation of AI tools are a long way short of perfect. These tools make mistakes, false connections, and they hallucinate. To master the use of the tools requires both the expertise to know what a good answer looks like and the vigilance to ensure it is delivered. Used properly, they relieve us of so many of the repetitive burdens we've grown used to carrying. Used wisely, they clear the decks, and gift us far greater focus.

In my experience, the greatest changes have come not from chasing new tools, but from mastering the new discipline of AI. It's a discipline rooted in leadership, learning, and planning that connects human insight and enhances it. To my mind, the future of business productivity is not the "man versus machine" scenario conjured by the naysayers, but a question of mastery enhanced by tools that serve us both as people and a society.

Enterprisation has always been about helping business leaders reclaim control, simplify complexity, and unlock performance without the personal cost. AI has simply added fuel to that mission. It's removed more of the friction; it has amplified what is possible.

The final gain is profound. When AI is working well, you find yourself with time – time to think, to create, and above all to enjoy the very life you set out to improve when you took the risk of starting your business in the first place.

These ideas aren't just theoretical. I have developed my own processes and experienced the impact of AI-enabled working in my own business. I have seen it transform the performance of other businesses I work with too.

One service I have long provided is a comprehensive review of a company's business plan and board reporting. It's a high-value, high-trust product. It requires experienced judgement, attention to detail, and a strong understanding of what good looks like at board level, and it has taken years of learning to develop. Historically, it took several days of work by seasoned professionals to produce and deliver; the cost to produce it, internally, was over £5,000.

I set out to redesign that offer completely, with AI embedded at the heart of the process – not to devalue it, but to reimagine how it could be delivered, without sacrificing rigour, reliability, or quality.

To do this, I had to return to first principles. What, precisely, did the client receive? What decisions were made easier? What problems were solved? What information did they rely on, and how did they consume it? Only by breaking the service into its essential parts could I then consider which elements could be delegated to an intelligent tool, and which required human intervention.

Then came the harder part: teaching the AI to think like a business analyst and understand the needs of leaders.

That might sound ridiculous, but it's exactly what effective prompting is. It isn't about asking a clever question. It's about constructing a thought process – creating a structure of cues, sequencing the logic, and refining the language so the AI begins to work with you, not just for you. This doesn't happen with a single prompt. It happens through iterative testing, calibration, and review.

Eventually, I developed a set of prompt workflows that allowed me to produce the key components of the board pack review. It included the analysis, the commentary, the visual structuring, and the recommendations – all of this in a repeatable, consistent way. My requirement was not perfection, but a highly effective structure for an analyst to polish.

The result? A service that once cost £5,000 to prepare now costs less than £200. The price to the client can remain the same, or it can come down; either way, the margin has been transformed. What's more, I can now serve more clients, more flexibly, without compromising their experience.

The greater win is that the product offer is not cheapened; on the contrary, it is strengthened. By building an intelligent process around my expertise, I've created something more scalable, more consistent, and more valuable to the client. It arrives faster, is easier to action and now comes with some of my own time – time that AI has freed up to allow me to help my clients directly.

This is the kind of change that becomes possible when AI is used not as a novelty, but as an instrument of design.

What made it possible wasn't the tool itself, but my decision to structure the work. I knew what excellent looked like. I learned how to best deconstruct the outcome into its component parts. I took the time to effectively train the AI through proper prompting rather than treating it as a magical box of answers.

People, being people, will assume the AI tool should do all this for them automatically. It won't. They will get a poor answer and assume "it doesn't work". Remember that old adage, "a poor workman always blames his tools"? My advice? Don't give up when the first answer is wrong (or worse, assume it to be right!) Clarify your thinking. Refine your process. Iterate your prompts.

Many people will use AI indiscriminately and produce work that sounds convincing but lacks substance. The greatest risk to us, individually and as society, is polished mediocrity. Misplaced confidence without clarity.

That's why my message has not changed with the advent of AI as a low-cost tool for the masses. It is always the same. You must know your craft. You must structure your thinking. And you must own the process. AI will not make your work better if you do not already know what better looks like.

For those employees who take the trouble to master the opportunity, the prize is extraordinary: a faster, more focused, more joyful way to work; and for entrepreneurs, a business that rewards both its clients and its owner with clarity, consistency, and freedom.

That's why I believe so deeply in this moment. Not because it's fashionable or trending, but because I've felt a new joy for myself. I'm seeing what is possible and I'm living it. I so badly want others – you – to feel that same sense of momentum, clarity and joy.

If that means being a passionate pensioner in a hurry, so be it. There are few better things to race towards than a life where your work is lighter, your results more meaningful, and your mind more free.

Freedom and joy in business aren't just ideals. With the right tools, and the right mindset, they're entirely within reach.

Tim Meadows-Smith

Tim Meadows-Smith is a serial entrepreneur and business renewal architect. He describes himself as a "passionate pensioner in a hurry" and is the creator of the Enterprisation methodology. During a career that has taken him from internationally scaling Häagen-Dazs to rescuing distressed start-ups, Tim has always believed business should serve life, and never the other way round.

Now focused on helping CEOs reclaim time, unlock productivity, and lead with clarity, Tim blends enterprise-class structure with human insight. He's a relentless learner, a lover of proper coffee, and an advocate for joy both at work and socially. His current work uses AI not to replace expertise, but to multiply it, giving leaders the confidence, rhythm, and systems to build businesses that run beautifully without running them into the ground.

He lives in the middle of Suffolk with Claire, who has been at his side for over fifty years. Together they enjoy the sea and are about a quarter way round the coastal path of England. Tim thinks deeply, writes freely, and always has time for a good conversation.

www.ingramcontent.com/pod-product-compliance
Lightning Source LLC
Chambersburg PA
CBHW021937190326
41519CB00009B/1047